ELFQUEST: THE GRAND QUEST

VOLUME THREE

ELFQUEST CREATED BY
WENDY &
RICHARD PINI

ELFQUEST: THE GRAND QUEST
VOLUME THREE

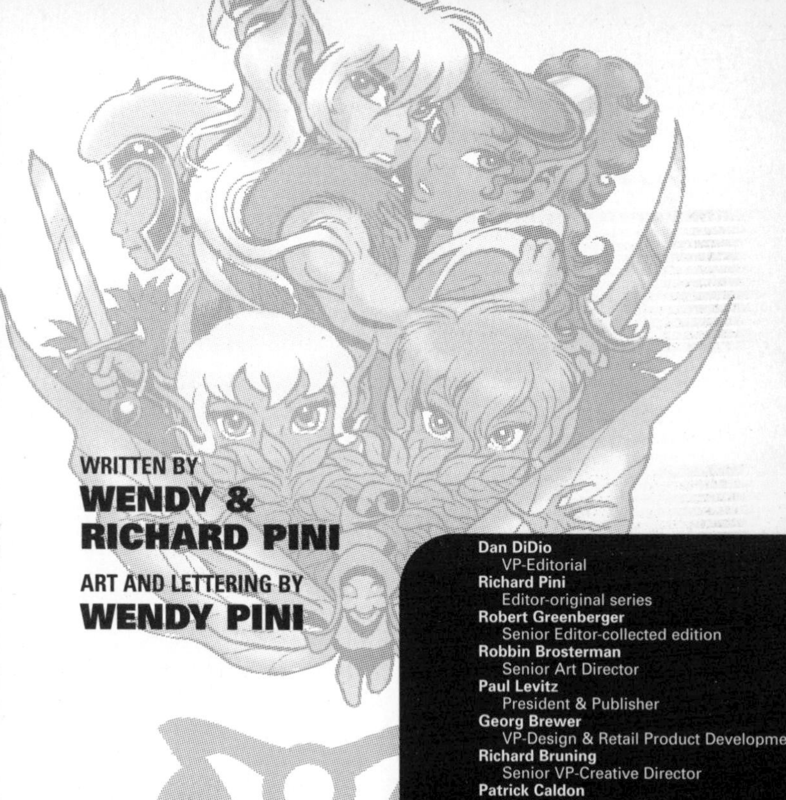

WRITTEN BY
WENDY & RICHARD PINI

ART AND LETTERING BY
WENDY PINI

ELFQUEST: THE GRAND QUEST VOLUME THREE
Published by DC Comics.

DC Comics, 1700 Broadway, New York, NY 10019
A Warner Bros. Entertainment Company
Printed in Canada. First Printing.
ISBN: 1-4012-0140-7

Cover illustration by Wendy Pini
Publication design by John J. Hill

The ElfQuest Saga is an ever-unfolding story spanning countless millennia that follows the adventures of humans, trolls and various elfin tribes. Some of the events that occur prior to the time of this volume are outlined below using the very first published ElfQuest story as a benchmark.

0

1,000

OUR STORY BEGINS HERE...

7 YEARS LATER

Recognition has given Cutter and Leetah twin children, Ember and Suntop, and the two tribes at last live in peace. The arrival of nomadic humans, though, alerts the elves to the continuing threat. Cutter and Skywise, seeking strength in numbers, set out to find other elfin tribes. Their journey leads them through the mysterious Forbidden Grove...

2,000

2,000 - 3,000 YEARS BEFORE

3,000

Goodtree, eighth chief of the Wolfriders, founds a new Holt deep in the woods and creates the Father Tree where the Wolfriders can all live. Her son, *Mantricker, i*s the first in several generations to have to deal with nomadic humans again.

Mantricker's son, *Bearclaw,* discovers Greymung's trolls who live in the caverns and tunnels beneath the Holt. Bearclaw becomes the Wolfriders' tenth chief.

In the distant Forbidden Grove near Blue Mountain, *Petalwing* and the preservers tirelessly protect their mysterious wrapstuff bundles.

Among the Wolfriders, *Treestump, Clearbrook, Moonshade, Strongbow, One-Eye, Redlance, Pike, Rainsong* and *Woodlock* are born.

4,000 YEARS BEFORE

4,000

Freefoot leads the Wolfriders during a prosperous time. Game is plentiful, and life is easy.

5,000

Freefoot's son, Oakroot, subsequently becomes chief and later takes the name *Tanner.*

6,000

9,000 YEARS BEFORE

Wolfrider chief Timmorn feels the conflict between his elf and wolf sides, and leaves the tribe to find his own destiny. *Rahnee the She-Wolf* takes over as leader, followed by her son *Prey-Pacer.*

7,000

10,000 YEARS BEFORE

8,000

Over time, the early High Ones become too many for their faraway planet to support. *Timmain's* group discovers the World of Two Moons, but as the crystalline ship approaches, the trolls revolt. The High Ones lose control and crash-land far in the new world's past. Ape-like primitive humans greet them with brutality, and the elfin High Ones scatter into the surrounding forest.

In order to survive, Timmain magically takes on a wolf's form and hunts for the other elves. In time, the High Ones adapt, making a spartan life for themselves. *Timmorn,* first chief of the Wolfriders, is born to Timmain and a true wolf.

9,000

10,000 YEARS BEFORE

10,000

TIMELINE

0
475
600
1,000
2,000
3,000
4,000
5,000
6,000
7,000
8,000
9,000
10,000

FIRE & FLIGHT

The peace is an illusion, and humans burn the Wolfriders from their forest home. Cutter and his band are driven into a vast desert where, at the end of their strength, they discover a second tribe of elves, the Sun Folk. Cutter recognizes the Sun Folks' healer Leetah, and the two groups unite in an uneasy alliance.

6 YEARS BEFORE

The feud between elves and humans ends – seemingly – with the death of Bearclaw. Cutter takes the chief's lock and assumes leadership of the tribe.

25 YEARS BEFORE

Joyleaf gives birth to a son, Cutter, who forms a fast friendship with Skywise. The two become brothers "in all but blood."

475 YEARS BEFORE

Bearclaw begins a long feud with a tribe of humans who have claimed the land near the Wolfriders' Holt. Though both sides suffer over the years, neither can prevail, and neither will give in.

600 YEARS BEFORE

In an oasis called the Sun Village deep in the desert to the south of the Holt, *Rayek* is born to villagers Jarrah and Ingen. *Leetah* is born to Suntoucher and Toorah twelve years later.

7,000 YEARS BEFORE

Swift-Spear, fourth chief, goes to war for the first time against the humans of a nearby village. The humans are forced to leave, and he earns the name *Two-Spear.*

Two-Spear has strange dreams of the humans returning and believes the elves are no longer safe. He becomes obsessed by the dreams and tries repeatedly to convince the Wolfriders they must wipe out the human threat for all time. When his sister Huntress Skyfire challenges his chieftainship, the tribe splits. Two-Spear leaves with his followers, and Skyfire becomes chief of the remaining tribe.

10,000 - 8,000 YEARS BEFORE

In a long diaspora, descendants of the High Ones wander the world. *Savah* and her family settle the Sun Village in the desert at Sorrow's End. Lord Voll and the Gliders move into Blue Mountain and shut themselves away from the world.

Guttlekraw becomes king of the trolls, who have fled to the cold north.

Ekuar and two rock-shaper companions discover the abandoned palace-ship of the High Ones but are enslaved by Guttlekraw. Glaciers force the trolls to move south, tunneling under the future Holt of the Wolfriders.

Greymung rebels against Guttlekraw. Guttlekraw and his cohorts return north, and the three rock-shaper elves escape in the melee.

Winnowill leaves Blue Mountain, finds the troll, seduces him and gives birth to *Two-Edge.* She later kills the troll.

The ElfQuest saga spans thousands of years and to date has introduced readers to hundreds of characters. At the time of the stories in this volume, these are the major characters you will meet and get to know.

THE ELVES

CUTTER

While his name denotes his skill with a sword, Cutter is not a cold and merciless death-dealer. Strong in his beliefs, he will nevertheless bend even the most fundamental of them if the well-being of his tribe is at stake. Skywise believes that what sets Cutter apart from all past Wolfrider chieftains is his imagination and ability to not only accept change, but take advantage of it.

LEETAH

Her name means "healing light" and – as the Sun Folks' healer – she is the village's most precious resource. For over 600 years she has lived a sheltered life, surrounded by love and admiration, knowing little of the world beyond her desert oasis. Though delicate-seeming, beneath her beauty lies a wellspring of strength that has yet to be tested.

EMBER

Named for her fire-red hair, Ember is destined to be the next chief of the Wolfriders. As such, she constantly watches and learns from her father's actions; she also learns gentler skills from Leetah. As Cutter was a unique blend of his own parents' qualities, so too is Ember. She shares a close bond with her twin brother Suntop, giving her strength.

SUNTOP

Suntop is the gentler, enigmatic son of Cutter and Leetah. Although a true Wolfrider, Suntop was born in the Sun Village and considers it home. Content that Ember will become chief of the Wolfriders, he says of himself, "I'll be what I'll be." Suntop has powerful mental abilities; his "magic feeling," as he calls it, alerts him when magic is being used by other elves.

SKYWISE

Orphaned at birth, Skywise is the resident stargazer of the Wolfriders, and only his interest in elf maidens rivals his passion for understanding the mysteries of the universe. Skywise is Cutter's counselor, confidant, and closest friend. While he is capable of deep seriousness, nothing can diminish Skywise's jovial and rakish manner.

TREESTUMP

Seemingly gruff and no-nonsense, Treestump also has a vulnerable side, especially when it comes to protecting the well-being of his tribemates. More than a thousand years of living with "the Way" has given Treestump a wellspring of wisdom, allowing him to find calm even in the face of great danger. He is something of a father figure to the entire tribe.

STRONGBOW

Strongbow is the reserved, silent master archer of the Wolfriders. Ever the devil's advocate, he is often proved right but finds no value in saying "I told you so." Strongbow is extremely serious, rarely smiles, and prefers sending to audible speech. He is completely devoted to his lifemate, Moonshade, and intensely proud of their son Dart.

NIGHTFALL

Nightfall is the beautiful counterpoint to her lifemate, Redlance, and one of the most skilled hunters in the tribe. She is cool and calculated, neither vengeful nor violent unless absolutely necessary. The relationship between Nightfall and Redlance is very much one of yin and yang. Nightfall grew up with Cutter and is strongly loyal to the young chief.

REDLANCE

Redlance is the sweet-natured plantshaper of the Wolfriders. Indeed, he will only use his talents defensively to protect the tribe. Redlance is too much a pacifist at heart to do willful harm, and this gentleness makes him a natural to care for the cubs of the tribe. Redlance is a master of the soft counsel, gently prodding other, more headstrong elves in the right direction.

MOONSHADE

Moonshade is the Wolfriders' tanner. Though the process can be lengthy and tedious, she enjoys the quiet hours spent bringing the beauty out of a supple hide. Moonshade, like her lifemate Strongbow, is very much a traditionalist, strong-minded and with unshakable beliefs. Completely devoted to her mate, Moonshade will defend him even when she knows he's wrong.

SCOUTER

Scouter has the sharpest eyes of all the Wolfriders. He is steadfast, loyal, and often overprotective. He is also extremely intolerant of anyone, tribemates included, whom he perceives as putting his loved ones in jeopardy. Dewshine and Scouter have been lovemates for most of their lives, yet are not Recognized.

ONE-EYE

Woodhue gained his new sobriquet after his right eye was put out by humans. Needless to say, this seeded a lifelong hatred and distrust of the "five-fingers." Although he still considers Cutter a cub, One-Eye never questions Cutter's judgments; Cutter is chief and that is that. One-Eye is fierce in battle, especially when his cub, Scouter, or his lifemate, Clearbrook, is endangered.

PIKE

Pike is the Wolfriders' resident storyteller, taking his name from his preferred weapon. The most ordinary and happy-go-lucky of the Wolfriders, Pike has no grand ideals or desires for quests – he is a follower and rarely questions his chief's orders. Fully immersed in "the now of wolf thought," he clings through thick and thin to his two greatest loves: dreamberries and taking the easy path.

SAVAH

By far the eldest elf known to either the Wolfriders or Sun Folk, Savah – the "Mother of Memory" for the village – is a child of the original High Ones who first came to the World of Two Moons. Infinitely wise and compassionate, she is the keeper of both history and ritual for the desert elves, yet all her years have not dimmed the twinkle of humor in her eyes.

OTHERS

PETALWING

Petalwing is a Preserver – a carefree, fairylike creature that arrived on the World of Two Moons with the original High Ones. Petalwing lives under the grand illusion that "highthings" (elves) cannot live without it, and must be watched over and protected. Petalwing is the closest thing that the Preservers have to a leader. Cutter considers Petalwing to be a major annoyance; the sprite is unperturbed by this.

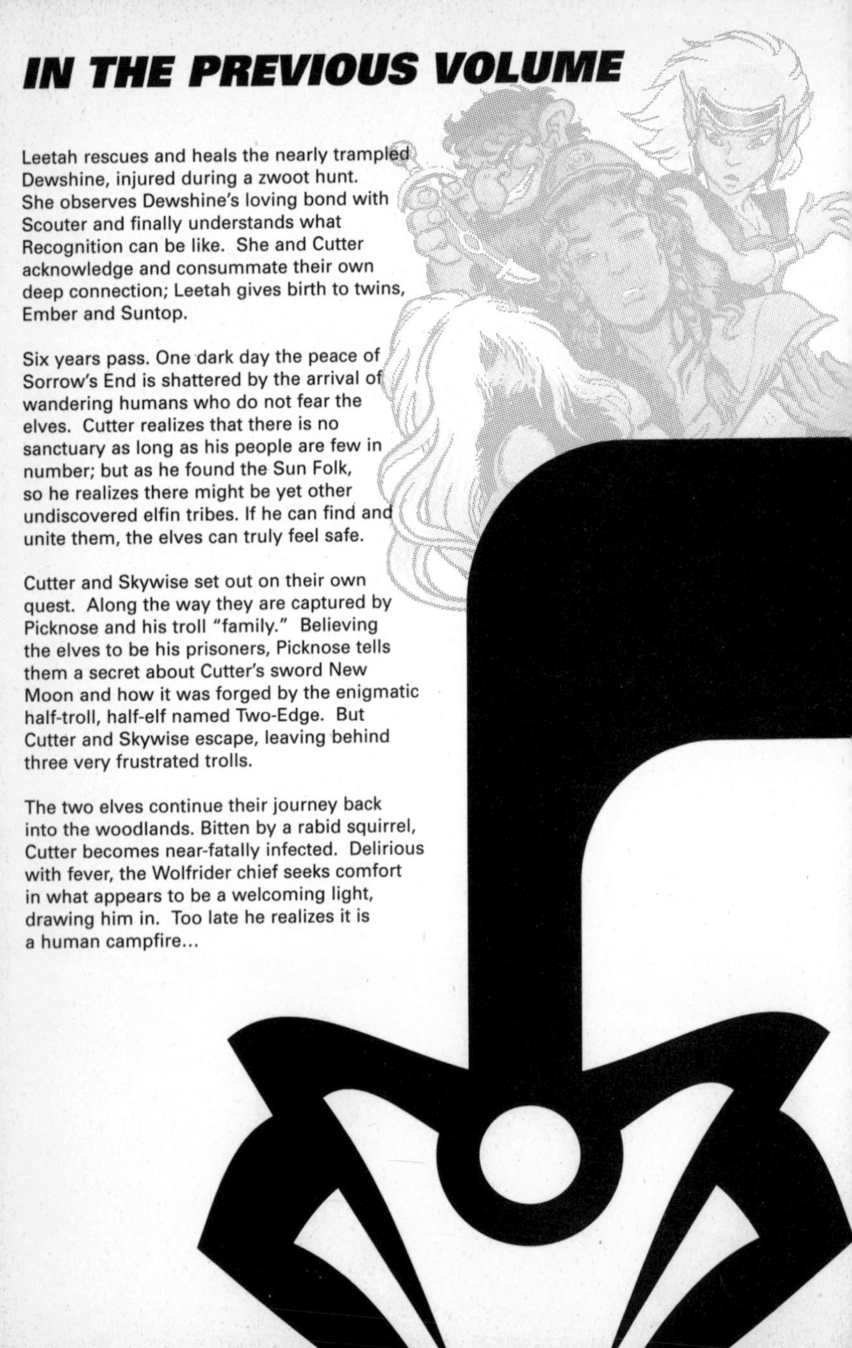

IN THE PREVIOUS VOLUME

Leetah rescues and heals the nearly trampled Dewshine, injured during a zwoot hunt. She observes Dewshine's loving bond with Scouter and finally understands what Recognition can be like. She and Cutter acknowledge and consummate their own deep connection; Leetah gives birth to twins, Ember and Suntop.

Six years pass. One dark day the peace of Sorrow's End is shattered by the arrival of wandering humans who do not fear the elves. Cutter realizes that there is no sanctuary as long as his people are few in number; but as he found the Sun Folk, so he realizes there might be yet other undiscovered elfin tribes. If he can find and unite them, the elves can truly feel safe.

Cutter and Skywise set out on their own quest. Along the way they are captured by Picknose and his troll "family." Believing the elves to be his prisoners, Picknose tells them a secret about Cutter's sword New Moon and how it was forged by the enigmatic half-troll, half-elf named Two-Edge. But Cutter and Skywise escape, leaving behind three very frustrated trolls.

The two elves continue their journey back into the woodlands. Bitten by a rabid squirrel, Cutter becomes near-fatally infected. Delirious with fever, the Wolfrider chief seeks comfort in what appears to be a welcoming light, drawing him in. Too late he realizes it is a human campfire...

DELIRIOUS FROM FEVER CAUSED BY AN INFECTED WOUND, **CUTTER** STAGGERS TOWARD THE OPEN FLAMES OF A CAMPFIRE AND PASSES OUT IN THE ARMS OF THE HUMAN WOMAN TENDING IT. MOMENTS LATER, **CUTTER'S** LOYAL WOLF **NIGHTRUNNER** CHARGES IN TO RESCUE HIS ELF-FRIEND.

HEARING HER SCREAM, SEEING HER DANGER, THE WOMAN'S MATE RUSHES TO THE FIRE AND SNATCHES UP A FLAMING BRAND...
BRAVELY HE FACES THE MADDENED WOLF, WAVING HIS TORCH IN AN EFFORT TO FRIGHTEN THE HUGE BEAST AWAY!

NIGHTRUNNER FIGHTS TO REACH CUTTER. HE WOULD KILL BOTH HUMANS IN AN INSTANT IF THE TERRIBLE FIRE DID NOT BLIND HIS GOOD EYE SO!
<NONNA! TAKE THE YOUTH INTO THE DWELLING -->
<-- QUICKLY!>
BACK, YOU MONSTER! GO AWAY!!
HA!
YIIIYIIYIIE!
SSSSSS

BURNED, TEMPORARILY BLIND AND IN AGONY, NIGHTRUNNER FLEES...

<I'D BEST KEEP WATCH TONIGHT -->

WHINE WHINE WHINE

<-- IN CASE THE BEAST RETURNS!>

OWWW!

HUH?!

<NONNA!>

<WHAT HAPPENED?>

<HE *CUT* ME! HE CUT ME WITH THAT STRANGE, *BRIGHT KNIFE!*>

THE MAN AND WOMAN STARE AT THE ELF IN BEWILDERMENT...
<DON'T COME ANY CLOSER!>
<HE SPEAKS OUR WORDS, BUT STRANGELY! I CAN BARELY UNDERSTAND HIM!>
<LOOK AT HIS *EYES*... THIS IS *NO CHILD*, NONNA!>
WARILY **CUTTER** EDGES HIS WAY AROUND THE HUMANS, NEW MOON DRAWN, THREATENING, READY TO SLASH AGAIN AT THEIR SLIGHTEST MOVE!

THE STRETCHED HIDE DOOR-COVERING IS ONLY A FEW STEPS AWAY...

<WE MUST STOP HIM! HE IS *MAD* FROM SICKNESS!>
<HE'LL *DIE* ALONE IN THE FOREST!>

THUP!
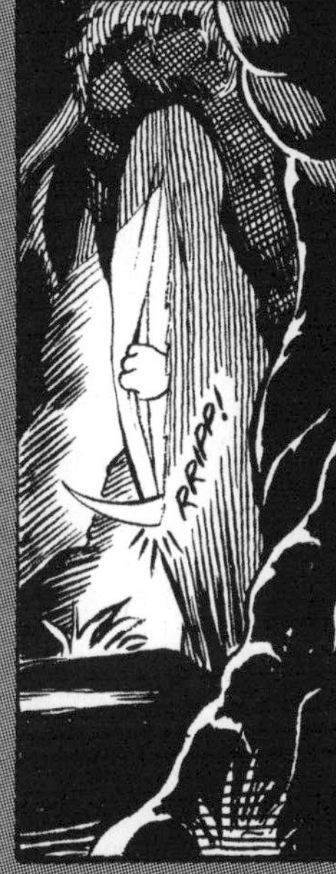
RRIPP!

CAPTURED -- BY HUMANS!

FOR NIGHTRUNNER THERE IS NO CHOICE BUT TO TRY TO OUTRACE DEATH!
RUN RUN BACKTRACK RUN SMELL THE WAY BACK --

-- BACK TO COLD WET WATER BACK TO MOSS BED BACK TO CUTTER FRIEND

-- STRONG SCENT CUTTER FRIEND OTHER SCENT OTHER FRIEND --

-- MUST FIND OTHER FRIEND --

-- MUST FIND HELP CUTTER FRIEND HELP RUN RUN...

FOCUSING ON THE PROBLEM AT HAND, SKYWISE HAS NOT DWELLED ON WORRISOME THOUGHTS OF HIS CHIEF.
HERE, STARJUMPER. THIS LOOKS LIKE THE PLACE TO FIND WHISTLING LEAVES!
KEEP YOUR EARS PRICKED...
THE RIGHT LITTLE BREEZE CAN SOMETIMES SHOW YOU WHERE THEY ARE!
IT'S TOO BAD ALL THESE TREES COVER UP THE STARS.
I COULD ALWAYS HUNT BETTER BY STARLIGHT!
OH, WELL...AT LEAST CUTTER'S SAFE WITH NIGHTRUNNER...
<THERE IS SUCH FEAR IN YOUR EYES, HONORED ONE!>
<NO NEED FOR FEAR...I KNOW WHO YOU ARE!>

IF A MORE HORRIBLE NIGHTMARE COULD BE DREAMED INTO LIFE, CUTTER DOES NOT KNOW WHAT IT MIGHT BE. HE WANTS TO LEAP FROM THE WOMAN'S ARMS, BUT HE IS TOO WEAK TO MOVE! THE THICK MAN-SCENT IS UNBEARABLE, AND IT IS MADE WORSE BY THE PAIN BLAZING WITHIN HIS INFECTED BODY.
WHY DON'T THEY KILL ME? HUMANS ALWAYS KILL ELVES WHEN THEY CATCH THEM!
WHAT'S SHE DOING...?
SPLISH
SPLISH

NEVER IN HIS LIFE HAS CUTTER BEEN CLOSER THAN A SWORD'S LENGTH TO A HUMAN.

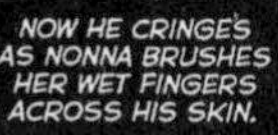

NOW HE CRINGES AS NONNA BRUSHES HER WET FINGERS ACROSS HIS SKIN.

SOFTLY SHE FANS HIM WITH THE LEAF, AND THE RESULTING BLESSED COOLNESS RELAXES THE ELF SOMEWHAT.

HUMANS AND NON-HUMAN SHARE A SILENCE THAT IS PREGNANT WITH COMPLEX EMOTIONS.

CUTTER'S EVERY INSTINCT WARNS HIM THAT HE IS IN DEADLY PERIL. BUT THE WOMAN'S SMILE IS GENTLE -- EVEN LOVING. AND THE MAN SEEMS MERELY PUZZLED, NOT FULL OF HATE.

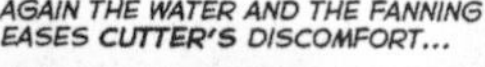

AGAIN THE WATER AND THE FANNING EASES CUTTER'S DISCOMFORT...

<I...DIDN'T KNOW -->
<-- THAT HUMANS COULD BE KIND...!>

<YOUR FOLK WERE ALWAYS GOOD TO MY PEOPLE, HONOED ONE. I -->
<OH! HE'S *ASLEEP* AGAIN! POOR LITTLE SPIRIT!>
NONNA, ARE YOU CERTAIN? I MEAN, IS THIS REALLY ONE OF -->
<-- THE *BIRD SPIRITS* FROM THE MOUNTAIN?>

<OF *COURSE* HE IS! SEE THE LONG, TAPERED EARS, LIKE WINGS? AND HERE -- THE *FOUR* FINGERED HANDS?>
<IS IT NOT JUST AS I HAVE SHOWN YOU IN THE *SYMBOLS?*>
<THIS IS ALL TOO *STRANGE* FOR ME!>

<OH *ADAR!* WHAT IF HE SHOULD *DIE* THROUGH SOME CLUMSINESS OF OURS?>
<ONLY *SPIRITS* CAN HEAL THEIR OWN!>
<*YOU* WORRY ABOUT THAT! *I'LL* MEND THE DOOR HIDE! THAT'S SOMETHING *I* CAN UNDERSTAND, AT LEAST!>
THE HUMANS TRADE GOOD NATURED SMILES, BUT THEY CANNOT HELP GLANCING NERVOUSLY AT THEIR UNCONSCIOUS CHARGE.

MEANWHILE...
NOTHING!
I MIGHT AS WELL LOOK FOR A SINGLE SILVER HAIR IN A WHITE WOLF'S COAT! CAN'T RECOGNIZE HALF THESE PLANTS!
AND THE OTHER HALF WOULDN'T CURE A FLEA BITE!
OOOOHHH... PUCKERNUTS!
I DON'T LIKE THIS PLACE...
...NOT AT ALL!
JUST AS SKYWISE DECIDES IT WOULD BE BETTER TO CONTINUE HIS SEARCH SOMEWHERE ELSE...
LISTEN!
WHHHEEEEEEEEEEEEEEEE

THE ANXIOUS ELF LEAPS FROM ISLAND TO ISLAND IN THE QUAKING BOG...
WHEEEEEEEE

UNTIL HE LOCATES THE SOURCE OF THE FAINT, WHISTLING SOUND...
HIGH ONES BLESS YOU, LITTLE BREEZE!
WHEEEEEEE

QUICKLY SKYWISE COLLECTS SOME OF THE LEAVES, PROUDLY DISPLAYING THEM TO STARJUMPER.
OOOOO
WHA -- ?
SNIFF

OOWWOOOooooo
NIGHTRUNNER!
WHAT ARE YOU DOING HERE?!

WHY... YOU'RE ALL *BURNED!* HOW COULD THIS HAVE HAPPENED ...UNLESS... *HUMANS!*

WAS IT HUMANS?!

WHUF!!

TIMMORN'S BLOOD!

NO MORE NEEDS SAYING. THE VALIANT OLD WOLF LEADS **SKYWISE** BACK THROUGH THE WOODS AT A DEAD RUN!

AND FINALLY...

SO THEY HAVE HIM IN *THERE*, EH? WAIT HERE, **NIGHTRUNNER.**

I...HOPE I SEE YOU AGAIN...!

PANT PANT WHEEZE

HMPH! I GUESS SPIRITS DON'T APPRECIATE THE VALUE OF A GOOD HIDE!
THERE! THAT FIXES IT!
SLASHHH!
AAH!
AYOOOAH!
GRRAAAR!

SKYWISE! DON'T KILL! DON'T!!

WHAT??! YOU'RE OUT OF YOUR HEAD!!

AM I...?

DO AS I SAY AND LET THE HUMANS BE!

THOUGH CUTTER IS OBVIOUSLY ILL AND WEAK, THE CLEAR TRUTH OF HIS SENDING CANNOT BE IGNORED. RELUCTANTLY, SKYWISE SENDS STAR-JUMPER OUT OF THE ROOM.

<ANOTHER ONE, NONNA! NEXT THEY'LL BE COMING OUT OF THE CAVE WALLS!>

I'M... SO GLAD TO SEE YOU!

DID THEY HURT YOU? I'LL CUT THEM DOWN TO OUR SIZE IF THEY DID!

NO...I DON'T UNDERSTAND IT, BUT THE WOMAN...SHE GAVE ME WATER! I-I'M STILL VERY HOT, THOUGH.
HERE! YOU CHEW THESE UP! THEY'LL DO THE TRICK!
CUTTER EATS AS MANY OF THE SOUR-TASTING LEAVES AS HE CAN STOMACH...
...AND SOON HE RISES GROGGI TO GO OUTSIDE
<STAY STILL! RIGHT WHERE YOU ARE!>
NOT FOR A MOMENT WOULD SKYWISE CONSIDER HIS DISTRUST OF THESE -- AND ALL OTHER -- HUMANS UNFAIR. HE HAS ONLY TO REMEMBER --
-- THE GRISLY DISPLAY OF WOLFRIDER SKULLS YELLOWING ATOP GOTARA'S PILLAR OF SACRIFICE...

...OR THE SHARPENED STAKE USED ON A TRIBESMAN WHO LATER, PROUDLY, BORE AS HIS BADGE OF SURVIVAL THE TRIBE NAME: ONE-EYE!
AND MOST PAINFUL OF ALL...A SIGHT BURNED INTO HIS INFANT BRAIN WHEN SKYWISE WAS JUST HOURS OLD...A RAFT OARED BY TWO YOUNG HUMANS...
...THE DARKNESS ...THE RIVER --
-- AND HIS MOTHER EYES-HIGH'S TEARFUL, FRIGHTENED FACE RECEDING IN THE MIST.
SHE GAVE HIM UP TO THE SWIFT CURRENT'S MERCY. THE WOLFRIDERS FOUND HIM, BUT FOR EYES-HIGH IT WAS TOO LATE.
SINCE THE HIGH ONES' TIME IT HAS BEEN SO...CHILD TORN FROM PARENT, FRIEND FROM FRIEND...
DESPITE CUTTER'S WORDS, SKYWISE CANNOT BELIEVE THAT THINGS WILL EVER CHANGE. THE BEARDED TALL ONE'S SCOWL SEEMS PROOF ENOUGH!

ADAR IS MORE THAN A LITTLE OUTRAGED AT BEING BOLDLY THREATENED IN HIS OWN HOME BY SUCH A **SMALL** ASSAILANT...

<**NONNA**, YOU HAVE SAID THAT I MUST BE **RESPECTFUL** -->
<-- BUT BIRD SPIRIT OR NOT, I'LL **BREAK HIM IN TWO** IF HE DOESN'T DROP THAT KNIFE!>

JUST THEN, **CUTTER** RETURNS, AND IT IS PLAIN THAT HIS BODY HAS RID ITSELF OF MUCH OF THE FEVER-INDUCING POISON.

IT IS ALSO PLAIN THAT HE IS **FURIOUS!**
<I'VE SEEN **NIGHTRUNNER.** DID **YOU** BURN HIM?>
<THE WOLF? I **HAD** TO!>

<HE WOULD HAVE TORN *NONNA* AND ME TO BITS!>

<YOU KNOW THAT!>

OLD FEARS AND HATREDS DIE HARD. THE ELF CHIEFTAIN STRUGGLES TO SUPPRESS THOUGHTS OF REVENGE. HE SPEAKS WORDS THAT NO WOLFRIDER HAS EVER SPOKEN TO A HUMAN BEFORE...

<I... UNDER-STAND.>

<YOU HELPED ME EARLIER. I WANT TO THANK YOU.>

NOT REALIZING THE SIGNIFICANCE OF **CUTTER'S** GRATITUDE, THE MAN AND WOMAN MERELY NOD. GLANCING PAST **NONNA'S** SHOULDER, **CUTTER'S** EYE IS CAUGHT BY STRANGE SPLASHES OF **COLOR** ON THE FAR WALL OF A TORCHLIT CHAMBER...

<WHAT'S BACK THERE?>

<IT IS THE ***ROOM OF SYMBOLS,*** HONORED ONE. WOULD YOU AND YOUR BRAVE GUARDSMAN LIKE TO SEE IT?>

WELL, "BRAVE GUARDSMAN"? *THESE* HUMANS AREN'T SO BAD!

....
I'D *RATHER* HATE THEM!

AS THEY ENTER THE LOW-CEILINGED ROOM, CUTTER AND SKYWISE ARE STRUCK BY THE SENSATION THAT THEY HAVE DISCOVERED YET ANOTHER PLACE WHERE TRACES OF ANCIENT ELFIN MAGIC LINGER.
I WISH MY LITTLE SUNTOP WERE HERE RIGHT NOW. HE COULD TELL FOR SURE IF THIS ROOM WAS SHAPED BY ELVES LONG AGO!
ELVES THAT SHAPE ROCK LIKE TREES...? IS THAT POSSIBLE?
I WONDER... COULD THOSE OLD SHAPERS HAVE BEEN PART OF A TRIBE THAT SAVAH'S FAMILY CAME FROM?
SO MANY QUESTIONS...AND THE ANSWERS ARE LOST AMID THE DIM, CHILDHOOD MEMORIES OF AN IMMENSELY AGED ELF.
NONNA USHERS THE PAIR TO A VIVIDLY COLORED WALL...
<MY PAINTINGS ARE VERY POOR COMPARED TO THE MASTER SYMBOL-MAKERS OF YOUR RACE, HONORED ONES. BUT PERHAPS YOU WILL RECOGNIZE YOUR HIGH MOUNTAIN HOME HERE, AS I HAVE SHOWN IT?>
<YOU SEE? I HAVE PAINTED A FLIGHT OF YOUR GIANT HUNTING BIRDS SOARING ABOVE THE BLUE PEAKS.>
<AND BETWEEN EACH BIRD'S WINGS RIDES A GALLANT SPEAR-BEARER!>
<UH... ULP WHERE IS THIS MOUNTAIN?>

⟨YOU TEST ME? I HAVE NOT FORGOTTEN!⟩
⟨MANY DAYS' WALK, IT IS... BEYOND THE WOODS...BEYOND THE VALLEY OF ENDLESS SLEEP.⟩
⟨WE MUST FOLLOW THE SETTING SUN UNTIL THE TALL, BLUE PEAKS COME INTO VIEW. BUT...⟩
⟨Y-YOU HAVE NOT COME TO TAKE ME BACK THERE, HAVE YOU, BIRD SPIRITS?⟩
⟨PLEASE DO NOT PART ME FROM ADAR!⟩
⟨US...? WHY, EH...NO!⟩
⟨WE'VE BEEN AWAY FROM THE MOUNTAIN FOR A LONG TIME, TOO...⟩

⟨HAVEN'T WE, SKYWISE?!⟩
⟨UH...YES!⟩
⟨SPIRIT BUSINESS, YOU KNOW...VERY SECRET!⟩
⟨IN FACT, WE'VE BEEN GONE SO LONG THAT WE'VE FORGOTTEN WHAT LIFE IN THE MOUNTAIN WAS LIKE!⟩
⟨ARE WE MUCH DIFFERENT FROM OUR KINFOLK WHO DWELL THERE NOW?⟩
⟨ONLY IN SIZE.⟩
⟨YOU SEEM SMALLER THAN THEY ARE.⟩

<"WELL, LONG JOURNEYS DO THAT TO SPIRITS,"> CUTTER WRYLY EXPLAINS. <"BUT WE PLAN TO GO HOME VERY SOON."> BARELY ABLE TO CONTAIN THEIR EXCITEMENT, THE ELVES KNOW THEY HAVE DISCOVERED THE GREATEST CLUE YET!
SKYWISE, IT MAKES SENSE! THESE HUMANS COULD BE TALKING ABOUT ELVES WHO ARE ALLIED WITH BIRDS --
-- JUST AS WE'RE ALLIED WITH WOLVES!
IF ONLY WE COULD BE SURE!

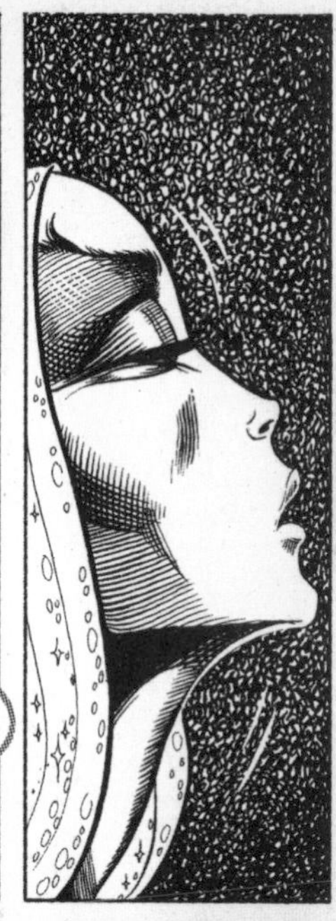

I DON'T KNOW, CUTTER... HUMANS ARE WICKED AND CRUEL! THEY LIE! WE'D BE FOOLS TO TRUST THEM!
THAT'S THE PAST TALKING! THE HUMANS WHO PLAGUED US IN THE HOLT WERE FULL OF HATE. BUT THOSE TWO AREN'T!
DON'T WORRY. MY EYES ARE OPEN. BUT THE WOMAN DID HELP ME! AND NOW SHE'S PUT US ON A PATH THAT MAY LEAD TO OTHER CHILDREN OF THE HIGH ONES!
THE TRAIL GROWS WARMER, MY FRIEND! WE'LL REST HERE 'TIL MY STRENGTH COMES BACK, THEN WE'LL SEE WHAT WE FIND!

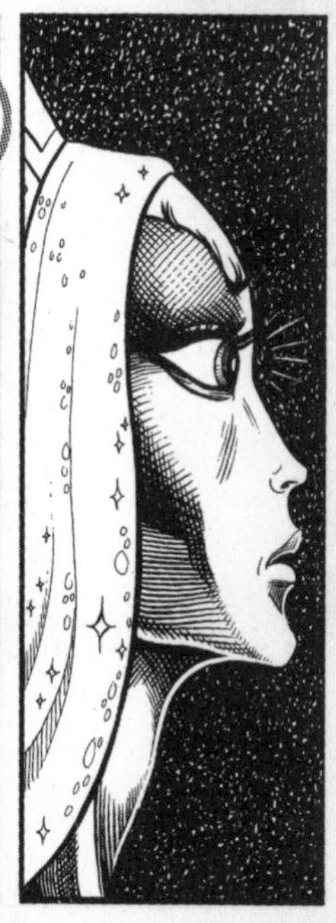

MEANWHILE...
LOOK AT YOUR DAUGHTER -- DOWN ON ALL FOURS JUST AS I PREDICTED!
WHEN SHE SPROUTS FUR AND A TAIL I'LL BEGIN TO WORRY!
LIKE *THIS*, *CHOPLICKER!* SMELL OUT THE TRAIL!
WHY, WHAT'S BOTHERING *SUNTOP?*
HM?
HAVE YOU EVER SEEN HIM LOOK SO *ODD?*
YOU'D THINK HE'D BEEN STRUCK BY THE *SUN!*

AW...HE'S JUST GOT HIS MAGIC FEELING AGAIN!
IS THAT WHAT'S TROUBLING YOU, MY SON?
NO! IT'S SAVAH! I KNEW SHE "WENT OUT" AGAIN TODAY, BUT SOMETHING'S WRONG!
SHE CAN'T COME BACK!
HEALER!
HEALER!!
COME QUICKLY!
HEADS TURN AS SAVAH'S HANDMAIDEN, AHDRI, RUSHES FROM HER HUT...
QUICKLY! THE MOTHER OF MEMORY NEEDS YOU!
WHAT'S HAPPENED?!

THE CIRCULAR ROOM OF AUDIENCE IS DARK. THE LIGHT BORN OF **SAVAH'S** ENERGY NO LONGER SHINES BEHIND HER THRONE.

GREAT SUN! SHE'S ALL BUT COMPLETELY ***LEFT HER BODY!***

BRING HER BACK, HEALER...OH, ***PLEASE BRING HER*** BACK!

THIS IS NOT AN *INJURY, AHDRI!*

I HAVEN'T THE POWER TO CALL BACK A SPIRIT THAT HAS TAKEN FLIGHT OF ITS OWN ACCORD!

SLOWLY, PURPOSEFULLY, SUNTOP CLIMBS ONTO THE MOTHER OF MEMORY'S LAP.

HE FLINGS HIS TINY ARMS AROUND HER VENERABLE SHOULDERS AND PRESSES HIS FOREHEAD TO HERS.

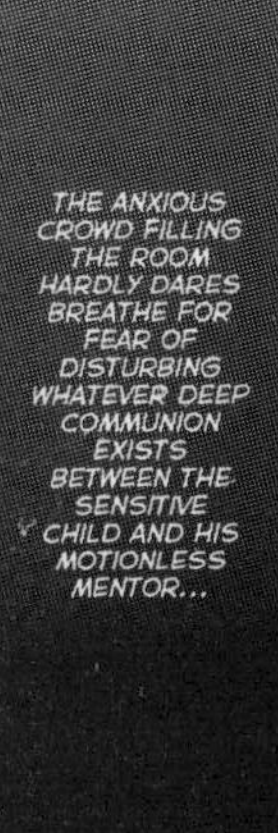
THE ANXIOUS CROWD FILLING THE ROOM HARDLY DARES BREATHE FOR FEAR OF DISTURBING WHATEVER DEEP COMMUNION EXISTS BETWEEN THE SENSITIVE CHILD AND HIS MOTIONLESS MENTOR...

FOR A LONG TIME SUNTOP IS UNNATURALLY STILL. LEETAH QUELLS THE URGE TO PLUCK HIM AWAY FROM SAVAH AND SHAKE THE LIFE BACK INTO HIM.
MOTHER...?
MOTHER?!
MY CUBLING?
I WENT TO SEE SAVAH, MOTHER...
IT'S DARK THERE, AND SCARY! SHE'S TRYING TO GET BACK! I TRIED TO HELP HER FIND HER WAY, BUT IT'LL TAKE HER A LONG TIME. SHE'S SO TIRED!
I BEGGED HER TO LEAVE OFF HER SEARCH FOR A WHILE.
EVER SINCE CUTTER WENT AWAY, SHE'S BEEN OBSESSED WITH GUIDING HIM SOMEHOW.

JUST BEFORE SHE "WENT OUT," SHE SAID SOMETHING EVIL HAD TOUCHED HER -- SOMETHING THAT *CUTTER* MUST NOT FIND!
I COULD NOT STOP ER! SHE *HAD* TO LEARN WHAT THE DANGER IS!
AND NOW...SHE MAY BE *LOST TO US!*

MOTHER, TAKE ME TO FATHER, *PLEASE!*
WHAT?!
PLEASE! I'VE GOT TO TELL FATHER WHAT *SAVAH* SEES -- I-I MEAN FEELS!
I'VE GOT TO *WARN* HIM!

CAN'T YOU TELL *US,* LITTLE CUB?
NO, *TREESTUMP!* ONLY *FATHER!*
IT'S ALL IN MY HEAD AND IT WON'T COME OUT 'TIL WE'RE WITH HIM!
BUT...WE DON'T KNOW WHERE HE IS!
SAVAH KNOWS WHERE HE *WILL* BE! WE STILL HAVE TIME TO GET THERE! I CAN SHOW YOU THE WAY! OH, MOTHER, *PLEASE!*

MANY EYES ARE ON LEETAH AS SHE TRIES TO SOOTHE HER CHILDREN'S DISTRESS. HER EARLIER WORDS HAUNT HER...
"I WAS AFRAID TO GO WITH CUTTER -- AFRAID!" NOW IT SEEMS SHE HAS NO CHOICE --
-- BUT TO SEEK HER LIFEMATE IN A LAND MORE FEARSOME THAN ANY LEGEND SHE KNOWS!

DIMLY ILLUMINATES THE SANDSTONE CAVES WHERE THE WOLFRIDERS PREPARE FOR A HAZARDOUS, BUT NECESSARY, JOURNEY...
THESE NEW LEATHERS ARE SOFT AS FLOWER PETALS, MOONSHADE! YOUR TANNING SKILLS ARE STILL UNMATCHED!
LOOK AT THOSE BROWN-SKINNED RABBITS! YAP YAP YAP! ALWAYS TALKING! NO ONE EVER JUST DOES ANYTHING AROUND HERE!
HAVE A LITTLE PITY, STRONGBOW!
WITH SAVAH BEYOND THEIR REACH AND LEETAH LEAVING THEM, THE SUN FOLK HAVE REASON TO BE STIRRED UP!
INDEED, LEETAH IS VERY MUCH AWARE OF HER PEOPLE'S CONSTERNATION AS SHE BIDS SAVAH A SILENT FAREWELL...
HOW CAN YOU LEAVE THE MOTHER OF MEMORY IN THIS STATE, HEALER? HER SPIRIT DRIFTS IN A PLACE WITHOUT TIME OR LIGHT! SHE EXHAUSTED HERSELF FOR YOUR LIFEMATE'S SAKE! YOU CANNOT DESERT HER NOW!
I CANNOT HELP HER, AHDRI!
NEITHER I NOR SUNTOP CAN RESTORE SAVAH'S SPIRIT TO HER BODY. BUT AT LEAST WE CAN HEED THE WARNING WHICH SHE SPENT HER STRENGTH TO BRING US.
IT IS CUTTER WHO NEEDS US, NOW, FOR WE CAN HELP HIM... WE MUST!

OUTSIDE SAVAH'S HUT, THE SUN TOUCHER STRIVES TO REASON WITH THE VILLAGERS..

THE MOTHER OF MEMORY HAS TOLD US, THROUGH AHDRI, THAT SOMETHING EVIL LIES IN CUTTER'S PATH --

-- SOMETHING THAT HE MUST NOT FIND!

MY DAUGHTER CHOOSES TO GO TO HER LIFEMATE'S AID!

WE HAVEN'T THE RIGHT TO HINDER HER!

ONLY SUNTOP CAN LOCATE HIS FATHER QUICKLY ENOUGH TO DELIVER THE WARNING IN TIME! THE SECRET OF THAT DANGER IS LOCKED WITHIN THE CHILD'S MIND.

ONLY WHEN FATHER AND SON ARE REUNITED CAN THE EVIL BE REVEALED.

UNCONVINCED, THE VILLAGERS PURSUE LEETAH AND HER FAMILY AS THEY WALK TO THE WOLFRIDERS' CAVES...

NO! DO NOT LEAVE US, HEALER!

WHAT IF SOMEONE IS INJURED WHILE YOU ARE GONE?

LET THE WOLFRIDERS TAKE CUTTER'S SON TO HIM!

NO! THE WOLFRIDERS MUST STAY, TOO!

THEY ARE OUR HUNTERS -- OUR PROTECTORS!

MUCH OF THIS IS MY FAULT!
BY SOOTHING EVERY LITTLE HURT WITH A TOUCH OR A WORD, I HAVE ENCOURAGED MY PEOPLE TO BE TOO DEPENDENT UPON ME! WE ARE ALL WEAKER FOR IT!

LEETAH'S LAST DOUBT FADES. SHE KNOWS, NOW, WHERE HER DUTY TRULY LIES AS SHE JOINS HER ARMED, LEATHER-CLAD ESCORTS.
WE'RE READY TO GO! AND MAY THE HIGH ONES GUIDE US AS NEVER BEFORE!
WAIT, LEETAH, PLEASE! WHAT IF THOSE HUMAN CREATURES COME AGAIN? WHAT IF MOUNTAIN LIONS DESCEND TO ATTACK US?
RAYEK USED TO GUARD THE VILLAGE BEFORE THE WOLFRIDERS TOOK HIS PLACE. WITH-OUT THEM, WE WILL BE DEFENSELESS!
GRRR!! GRUFF!!
NO YOU WON'T -- BECAUSE I'M GOING TO STAY AND TEACH YOU HOW TO FIGHT FOR YOURSELVES!
GASP DART!
THE YOUNG ELF BRAVELY FACES A SCOWLING STRONGBOW...
FATHER, I - I WANT TO DO THIS -- I HAVE TO! I GREW UP HERE IN SORROW'S END!

YOU?! A SPINDLY, HALF-GROWN YOUTH WILL BE OUR CHIEF HUNTER AND PROTECTOR?
AH! WE ARE LOST!
SUDDENLY, A STRANGE, HOARSE VOICE GROWLS AT THE VILLAGERS...
THAT "SPINDLY YOUTH" IS MY SON!
?!
AND HE'S WORTH THE LOT OF YOU PUT TOGETHER! HE CAN TEACH YOU TO HUNT AND TO FIGHT!
IT'S YOUR OWN HIDES IF YOU'RE TOO FANCY TO LEARN!

MOTHER! FATHER! THANK YOU! I WAS SURE YOU'D DISAPPROVE!
I DO!
YOU'RE WASTING YOUR TIME ON THESE SHIVERING FAWNS -- BUT IT'S YOUR DECISION. JUST REMEMBER, YOU'RE A WOLFRIDER! DON'T EVER FORGET WHERE YOU CAME FROM!
DON'T WORRY ABOUT YOUR PEOPLE, LEETAH. EVEN IF YOUR JOURNEY TAKES YOU AWAY FOR MANY SEASONS --
-- THE VILLAGE WILL HAVE A HEALER! MY FATHER, RAIN, HAD POWERS SIMILAR TO YOURS. IN THIS LITTLE ONE COMING THEY FLOW AGAIN. I HAVE SENSED IT!
SNIFF
RAINSONG... YOU ARE A WONDER!
SEE, WING? CHOP-LICKER'S GOING WITH US!

I HOPE SO, MY LITTLE SISTER!
OH, LEETAH! WILL WE EVER SEE YOU AGAIN?
NO! DO NOT EVEN HINT THAT SOMETHING MIGHT HAPPEN!
I COULDN'T BEAR IT!
HUSH...
FIRST RAYEK AND NOW YOU, MY KITLING. THIS GOES AGAINST THE VERY PURPOSE OF THE VILLAGE!
I MUST GO, MOTHER! I CANNOT RETURN TO THE HALF-AWAKE LIFE I LED BEFORE CUTTER CAME TO ME! HE IS LIFE --
-- AND THIS IS MY AWAKENING!

WITH TIME'S PASSING, MANY CHANGES HAVE TAKEN PLACE. DEATH HAS ENDED SOME OLD BONDS BETWEEN ELF AND WOLF WHILE BIRTH HAS CREATED NEW ONES. BUT ONE SHARED JOY REMAINS CONSTANT -- THE HOWL!

YET THE SUN FOLK ARE NOT JOYFUL. THEIR FAREWELLS ARE MUTED AND HESITANT. CONCERN FOR THE TRAVELERS' SAFETY MINGLES WITH AN UNPLEASANT FEELING OF APPREHENSION...

FORGIVE ME, MY PEOPLE, IF OUR LEAVING DISTRESSES YOU. PLEASE WISH US A SAFE JOURNEY AND PRAY WE FIND CUTTER IN TIME!
THERE IS NO SAFETY FOR OUR KIND ANYWHERE BUT IN SORROW'S END!
AND NO PEACE FOR LEETAH ANYWHERE BUT WITH CUTTER!
HE HAS GIVEN HER A TASTE OF THE BITTERSWEET NECTAR OF RISK.
I DOUBT THAT WE SHALL SEE HER AGAIN UNTIL SHE HAS DRAINED THE CUP!

DEEP AMONG THE HUMID SHADOWS OF AN ANCIENT, MOSS-GARLANDED FOREST, A HOVEL THAT IS PART CAVE, PART HOLLOW TREE SERVES AS HOME FOR TWO SOLITARY HUMANS, NONNA AND ADAR.

EMANATING FROM THE HUMBLE DWELLING IS A FAINT, MAGICAL AURA... UNMISTAKABLY ELFIN MAGIC!

CUTTER, CHIEF OF THE WOLFRIDERS, IS FASCINATED BY THIS EVIDENCE OF HIS DISTANT ANCESTORS' TRAVELS.

<HOW DID YOU AND YOUR MATE COME TO LIVE HERE ALL ALONE, NONNA?>

THE WOMAN SHYLY LOWERS HER EYES, EMBARRASSED BY THE ELF'S STREADY, PENETRATING GAZE.

<WE ARE EXILES FROM THE TRIBE OF OLBAR THE MOUNTAIN-TALL. HE TOLD US WE COULD LIVE IN THE DEEP FOREST AS LONG AS WE NEVER CAME BACK TO THE VILLAGE AGAIN.>
<WHEN WE FOUND THIS PLACE, I LIKED IT AT ONCE. IT REMINDED ME, SOMEHOW, OF THE MOUNTAIN WHERE MY TRIBE LIVES TO SERVE THE BIRD SPIRITS -->
<-- SPIRITS LIKE YOU, HONORED ONE!>
DOES SHE MEAN ELVES?
BIRD RIDERS?
SKYWISE AND I MUST FIND THAT MOUNTAIN!

WHILE NONNA SPEAKS AMIABLY ENOUGH WITH CUTTER, HER MATE, ADAR, HAS GREATER DIFFICULTY "COMMUNING WITH THE SPIRITS..."
<I KNOW YOU'RE THERE! ANSWER ME!>
<I WON'T GO AWAY UNTIL YOU DO!>

<WELL...WHAT IS IT?>
<NONNA SAYS YOU BIRD SPIRITS CAN WORK MAGIC...>
<SHE SAYS YOU SPEAK ANIMAL LANGUAGE AND NEVER AGE. WELL THEN, TELL ME WHAT GOOD WILL COME TO ME IF I WORSHIP YOU!>
HUH?!
<"YES,"> CONTINUES ADAR. <"IF I MAKE THE PROPER SACRIFICES AND PLEASE YOU WITH SONGS OF PRAISE --">
< -- WILL YOU GRANT A FAVOR? NOT FOR ME -- FOR NONNA!>
<WHAT DO YOU WANT?>
<THIS PART OF THE FOREST HAS BEEN OUR HOME FOR AS MANY SNOWS AS I HAVE FINGERS. I DON'T MIND NEVER SEEING MY TRIBEFOLK -- THEY CAN GO FISH UP A TREE FOR ALL I CARE!>
<BUT NONNA IS LONELY.>
HE DOESN'T OMPLAIN -->
<-- BUT I KNOW SHE'D LIKE TO HAVE PEOPLE AROUND HER AGAIN. CAN YOU DO SOMETHING ABOUT IT?>
<WE HAVE NOTHING TO DO WITH HUMANS!>
<OH? SEEMS TO ME YOU HAVE EVERYTHING TO DO WITH NONNA -->
<-- ESPECIALLY SINCE SHE HELPED YOUR COMPANION WHEN HE WAS SICK!>
<BUT MAYBE YOU'RE TOO HIGH ABOVE US -->
<-- TO BE GRATEFUL!>

LATER, AS CUTTER AND SKYWISE REFRESH THEMSELVES IN THE COLD, CLEAR WATER OF A SECLUDED POND...
...SO NONNA TOLD ME HER MATE FOUND HER BY FOLLOWING A LONG RIVER THAT FLOWS BY HIS VILLAGE DOWN THROUGH THE VALLEY OF ENDLESS SLEEP --
-- WHATEVER THAT IS!
ANYWAY, THE RIVER LED ADÄR RIGHT TO THE FOOT OF THE "BIRD SPIRITS'" MOUNTAIN!

HUMANS ALWAYS CALL OUR KIND "SPIRITS" OR "DEMONS," DON'T THEY? JUST THINK! IF NONNA'S BIRD SPIRITS ARE ELVES --
-- THAT MEANS THEY'VE LIVED IN PEACE WITH HER TRIBE FOR MOONS WITHOUT NUMBER!
OWL PELLETS! HUMANS AND ELVES CAN'T LIVE TOGETHER!

THEN HOW DO YOU EXPLAIN NONNA?
MOON MADNESS...
BAD FOOD...
...WHO KNOWS?

I THINK WE SHOULD HELP THOSE TWO HUMANS GET BACK INTO THEIR VILLAGE. THE SOONER WE FIND THAT RIVER, THE SOONER WE CAN FOLLOW IT TO THE BIRD SPIRITS!
??!

WHAT??!
THAT DOES IT!!
THAT FEVER BURNED UP YOUR BRAINS!
SPLOSH!
HELP HUMANS?!!
WALK RIGHT INTO A NEST OF THEM?! WHY NOT TAKE NEW MOON AND CUT OFF YOUR OWN HEAD...? IT'S THE SAME THING!
COME ON! THAT'S JUST THE WAY BEARCLAW USED TO TALK! HUMANS KNOW THINGS THAT ARE IMPORTANT TO OUR QUEST!
AND IF WE'RE CLEVER AND CAREFUL, WE CAN LEARN EVEN MORE!

SKYWISE STARES AT HIS CHIEF AND FRIEND AND FOR THE FIRST TIME HE REALIZES WHAT IT IS THAT SETS CUTTER APART FROM BEARCLAW...FROM ALL THE PAST WOLFRIDER CHIEFTAINS --

-- IT IS IMAGINATION... AND THE ABILITY NOT ONLY TO ACCEPT CHANGE, BUT TO TAKE ADVANTAGE OF IT.

MEANWHILE, WHITE-HOT CLAWS OF LIGHTNING SLASH AT THE DISTANT HORIZON, BRIEFLY OUTLINING THE BILLOWING THUNDERHEADS WHICH TOWER IN THE VAST NIGHT SKY...

K--K--KRAKOW!

LEETAH HAS WITNESSED STORMS OF SUCH FEROCITY BEFORE, BUT ALWAYS FROM THE SNUG CONFINES OF HER STURDY HUT...

-- NEVER IN THE MIDDLE OF NOWHERE, WITH NO SHELTER IN SIGHT!
RRRRUUMBLE!
KRAK!
DON'T BE AFRAID, MOTHER!
I - I'M NOT!
AND NEITHER IS CH-CHOPLICKER!
THAT WAY, MOTHER! TURN THAT WAY OR WE'LL GET LOST!
EVEN WITHOUT SKYWISE AND HIS LODESTONE, I KNOW WE'RE NOT HEADED BACK OVER THE SAME GROUND THAT LED US TO SORROW'S END!
WHERE'S SUNTOP TAKING US, I WONDER?
HE SAID SOMETHING ABOUT A RIVER...BUT I DON'T CARE WHERE WE'RE GOING! ANYTHING'S BETTER THAN THIS TREELESS WASTE!
BESIDES, IT'LL BE GOOD TO SEE CUTTER AGAIN!
IF WE EVER DO SEE HIM, ONE-EYE ...IF!

BUT **CUTTER** AND **SKYWISE**, UNAWARE THAT THEIR FELLOW WOLFRIDERS HAVE SET OUT TO FIND THEM, HAVE AGREED TO HELP THE BANISHED HUMAN COUPLE REJOIN THE TRIBE OF **OLBAR THE MOUNTAIN-TALL. NONNA** LOOKS BACK WISTFULLY AT HER HOME OF MANY YEARS, BUT **ADAR** IS FILLED WITH FIERCE CONFIDENCE AND MOUNTING ANTICIPATION...

<THIS IS ***WELL!***>

<THE ***BONE WOMAN*** WILL ***HAVE*** TO BACK DOWN AND ACCEPT US ONCE SHE SEES WE'RE UNDER THE PROTECTION OF ***GOOD SPIRITS.***>

<***BONE WOMAN?***>

<MY TRIBE'S ***SHAMANESS!***>

<SHE SPOKE AGAINST ME WHEN I CAME BEFORE ***OLBAR*** TO PRESENT ***NONNA*** AS MY BRIDE. THE ***BONE WOMAN*** SAID ***NONNA*** WAS AN OUTSIDER FROM A LAND OF ***EVIL DEMONS!*** IT DIDN'T HELP MATTERS THAT ***NONNA*** WAS A SYMBOL-MAKER!>

<THE SHAMANESS CONVINCED MY CHIEF THAT I HAD BROUGHT ***BAD MAGIC*** INTO THE VILLAGE. I'M SURE ***OLBAR*** STILL LISTENS TO THAT OLD HAG.>

<SHE KNOWS HOW TO PLAY ON HIS ***FEARS!*** HE -->

SUDDENLY ADAR STOPS SHORT, GLANCING ABOUT IN PUZZLEMENT...
<THIS WOOD IS ALWAYS SO CURSED DARK! AND THE OLD PATHS I USED TO KNOW ARE CHANGED...OVERGROWN! IT'S BEEN A LONG TIME. I-I'M NOT SURE OF THE WAY!>
<I AM!>
THE LODESTONE SPINS TO A STOP, ITS LEFT SIDE FACING SUN-GOES DOWN, THE DIRECTION IN WHICH ADAR'S VILLAGE LIES...
<IT'S - IT'S MAGIC!!>
THOUGH HIS MISTRUST OF HUMANS IS STILL VERY DEEP, SKYWISE IS SECRETLY PLEASED THAT HIS TREASURED TALISMAN INSPIRES SUCH AWE...
<YES.. MAGIC! OF A VERY SPECIAL KIND!>
<THE LODESTONE KNOWS WHERE WE WANT TO GO AND IT WILL GUIDE US THERE WITHOUT FAIL!>
NONNA NODS AND SMILES UNQUESTION-INGLY, FOR HER FAITH IN THE "SPIRITS" IS ABSOLUTE.

SO A WOODLAND TREK OF MANY DAYS BEGINS...
THE JOURNEY IS A STRENUOUS ONE FOR THE HUMANS AS THEY TRY TO KEEP PACE WITH THEIR SEEMINGLY TIRELESS ELFIN GUIDES.
WHEN NONNA AND ADAR MUST SLEEP, THE TWO ELVES "WOLF NAP," KEEPING ALTERNATE WATCH FOR NIGHT PROWLING PREDATORS...
IT'S SO STRANGE...
WE CAN NEVER BE FRIENDS WITH HUMANS --
-- YET HERE WE ARE PROTECTING THEM!
AFTER AN EIGHT-OF-DAYS PASSES, AND MOTHER MOON HAS GONE THROUGH HALF HER CYCLE...
<THANK YOU, SPIRITS! I RECOGNIZE THESE TALL TREES. I'M SURE I CAN FIND MY VILLAGE NOW, WITHOUT THE AID OF YOUR MAGIC STONE!>
<GOOD! THEN WE'LL FOLLOW YOU!>
<FRIGHTENED...?>
<NOT NOW! NOT WITH THE GENTLE BIRD SPIRITS WATCHING OVER US...>
<...AND YOU BESIDE ME!>

THE MAN AND WOMAN TRAVEL ON, SUSTAINING THEMSELVES WITH SMALL GAME AND SOUR SHRUB BERRIES...
<HAVE OUR LITTLE HELPERS ABANDONED US, NONNA? WHERE ARE THEY?>
:CHUCKLE: <IN THE TREES! WHERE ELSE WOULD BIRD SPIRITS BE?>
RRRRRAAAAARR!
SNARL!
:GASP!:

WWHHHISSSHHH!
THAK!
WUUGH!
<ADAR...?>
<BY THE RIVER GOD'S TAIL!>
<I GOT IT IN THE PAW!>
<WHAT KILLED THE BEAST?>
GASP!
<LOOK! TWO ARROWS!>
<THE SPIRITS' DARTS ARE CHARMED!>
<THEY NEVER MISS THEIR MARK!>

OOOOOOOOWWWWOOOOOOOOOOOOO
<LISTEN! THEY CALL THEIR WOLF COMPANIONS TO FEAST ON THE KILL!>
<UH... NONNA...>
<L-LET'S LEAVE THEM TO FEED IN PEACE! WE'LL THANK THE SPIRITS -->
< --LATER!>
BY LATE AFTERNOON THE WAY-WORN COUPLE COME TO THE EDGE OF THE FOREST WHERE WOMEN FROM ADAR'S VILLAGE BEND TO THEIR CUSTOMARY TASKS...
OH!
<WHO ARE THEY?!>
<WHY...IT'S ADAR AND HIS OUTLANDER WOMAN! THEY'VE COME BACK!>

WITH SEEMING FEARLESSNESS, THE TWO EXILES STRIDE INTO THE VILLAGE...
<I AM ADAR, SON OF TOLF, THE WOOD-CLEAVER! MY WIFE, NONNA, AND I -->
<-- HAVE COME HERE SEEKING AN END TO OUR UNJUST BANISHMENT!>
BEFORE ADAR CAN SAY MORE, A HIDEOUS SHRIEK RENDS THE AIR AND A GROTESQUE FIGURE BURSTS THROUGH THE THRONG!
EVIL!! EVIL!!
EVIL IS HERE!!
<THE BONE WOMAN!>
YARK! YARK!

RATTLE!
KLAK!
<BAD MAGIC! FOUL MAGIC! CONSORTERS WITH DEMONS!! KILL THEM, AS YOU SHOULD HAVE DONE LONG AGO!>
<KILL THEM!!>
LIKE SPARKS TO DRY LEAVES, THE SHAMANESS' WORDS IGNITE HER PEOPLES' HATE! BUT AS THE FRENZIED CROWD CLOSES IN, THE PIERCING SOUND OF A HUNTING HORN DISTRACTS THE WOULD-BE EXECUTIONERS.
<DEMON LOVERS!>
TAAROOOOOOOO
<IT IS OLBAR!>
<NOW, OUTCASTS, YOU ARE TRULY DOOMED!>

HE STANDS A FULL HEAD TALLER THAN HIS TALLEST WARRIOR...HIS CHEST IS AS BROAD AS THAT OF THE FLATLAND BULL WHOSE HIDE HE WEARS...AND HIS EYES ARE AS HARD AS FLINT ARROWHEADS!
<SO, ADAR, IT SEEMS EXILE AGREES WITH YOU! OR HAS YOUR WOMAN CONJURED DEMONS TO TEND YOU ALL THIS TIME?>
<I DO NOT DENY THAT THE SPIRITS COMMUNE WITH NONNA!>
<THEN YOU MUST KNOW YOUR RETURN HERE MEANS YOUR DEATH!>
<WE GAMBLED ON YOUR WISDOM, MY CHIEF. IT IS NOT WISE TO DESTROY THOSE WHOM THE GOOD SPIRITS FAVOR!>
<THERE IS NO SUCH THING AS A GOOD SPIRIT!>
<I KNOW!>

<PLEASE LISTEN, GREAT CHIEF! I SWEAR ON MY LIFE'S BLOOD THAT I MEAN NO HARM!>
<LIKE THE WEATHER OR THE MIGHTY RIVER, THE SPIRITS I SERVE CAN BE AS TERRIBLE AS THEY ARE BEAUTIFUL. BUT THEY ARE GOOD!>
<WE CANNOT DENY THEM -- ANY OF US!>
<DO NOT BE DECEIVED, OLBAR!>
<THIS CHILDLESS ONE DOES NOT KNOW HER PLACE! SHE DARES TO MAKE SYMBOLS LIKE A MAN -- AND SUCH SYMBOLS! STRANGE AND EVIL! LOOK...! THE TOOLS OF HER VILE CRAFT ARE IN THIS POUCH!>
SNAP!
<THESE TWO REEK OF FOUL MAGIC! THEIR TONGUES ARE BERRY-SWEET, BUT THEIR HEARTS ARE FULL OF POISON THORNS!>
<KILL THEM!>
OLBAR IS LARGE AND POWERFUL, BUT SO ARE HIS FEARS. HIS HEART HOLDS NO SYMPATHY FOR WAYS AND BELIEFS DIFFERENT FROM HIS OWN.

<NO MORE TALK! THE BONE WOMAN SPEAKS TRUE!>
<OUTCASTS, YOU MUST DIE!>
<SLAY THEM, WARRIORS!>
<SLAY TH--!>
<BY THE FALLING DEATH WATER...!>

HUMAN EYES BULGE, HUMAN MOUTHS GAPE AT THE EERIE SIGHT OF CUTTER AND SKYWISE MOUNTED ON THEIR HUGE WOLVES.
OOOOHH...
<S-SPIRITS...! SAVE US!!>

<HEAR ME, HUMANS! YOU MUST ALLOW NONNA AND ADAR TO DWELL AMONG YOU, FOR THEY HAVE EARNED THE BIRD SPIRITS' ETERNAL FAVOR! ACCEPT THESE TWO EXILES INTO YOUR TRIBE AND GOOD FORTUNE IS YOURS!>

<HARM THEM AND THE SPIRITS WILL TAKE TERRIBLE REVENGE!>

WELL PLAYED! NOW CAN WE LEAVE?
BE PATIENT, SKYWISE! WE'RE NOT THROUGH YET!
<THIS MEAT OF THE FOREST WE GIVE YOU IN TOKEN OF OUR GOOD FAITH!>
"GOOD FAITH?!" HOO! HOW LONG CAN WE KEEP SPOUTING THIS SWAMP ROT?
GAAAH!!
<BEGONE, I COMMAND YOU, BEAST-EARED DEMONS! TURN YOUR EVIL EYES AWAY FROM US!>
RATTLE!
I - IS IT A TROLL?
CAN'T BE! TROLLS AREN'T THAT UGLY!
CLATTER!
<STOP, WOMAN!>
<HAVE YOU GONE MAD?!>
<WOULD YOU BRING THE WRATH OF ALL THE SPIRIT WORLD UPON US?>
<WHO RULES YOU HUMANS -- THAT BAG OF RATTLING BONES OR OLBAR THE MOUNTAIN TALL?>
<I - I AM OLBAR!>
<THEN TELL YOUR PEOPLE TO ACCEPT NONNA AND ADAR NOW AND FOREVER!>
<I WILL!>
OOF!
<NO, OLBAR! DRIVE THE BEAST-EARED ONES AWAY!>

<SILENCE, OLD ONE!>

<YOU FORGET THAT I HAVE BEEN TO THE *FORBIDDEN GROVE!*>

<I HAVE TASTED THE SPIRITS' VENGEANCE ONCE -->

<-- AND THAT WAS *ENOUGH!*>

<B-BUT *THESE* ARE OF MORE ANCIENT AND EVIL STOCK THAN THE *LITTLE WINGED ONES!*>

"FORBIDDEN GROVE?" "LITTLE WINGED ONES?" THERE'S MORE HERE TO LEARN THAN I THOUGHT!

UH OH!

<*STAY,* GRACEFUL SPIRITS!>
<HONOR *MY* HUMBLE VILLAGE WITH YOUR PRESENCE! TOMORROW WE WILL MAKE A *GREAT FEAST* FROM YOUR GIFT OF *SACRED MEAT!*>

AFTER TEN NIGHTS OF HARD TRAVELING AND TEN DAYS OF HIDING FROM THE SUN BENEATH A HEAVY, SILKEN TENT...
YOU'VE SEEN THESE BIG ROCKS BEFORE, TREESTUMP?
AYE, EMBER...SEVEN TURNS OF THE SEASONS AGO! BUT I SAW A DIFFERENT PART OF 'EM IN A DIFFERENT PLACE!
INSIDE THE TENT THE WOLFRIDERS EAT AND DRINK SPARINGLY OF THEIR DWINDLING SUPPLIES.
IF ONLY SUNTOP COULD TELL US MORE ABOUT WHERE WE'RE GOING! WE'VE GOT TO GET OUT OF THIS DESERT SOON!
THE CUB CAN'T REALLY UNDERSTAND --
-- WHAT IT'S LIKE TO SUFFER IN THIS WILDERNESS!
SO WE LEFT THE TUNNEL OF GOLDEN LIGHT AND STARTED ACROSS THE SANDS. MIND YOU, WE HAD NO FOOD, NO TENT AND PRECIOUS LITTLE WATER!
YOUR FATHER LED US FOR THREE DAYS THROUGH HEAT AND THIRST! HE WOULDN'T GIVE UP --
-- EVEN WHEN MOST OF US WERE READY TO!
OH!
LOOK! OVER THERE!
THERE'S A LITTLE CAVE IN THE CLIFF SIDE!

CAREFUL, SHE-CUB! WATCH OUT FOR SNAKES!
oOo!

THERE'S NO SNAKES IN HERE, TREESTUMP! BUT I SURE SMELL SOMETHING!

TREESTUMP SENDS FOR THE OTHERS TO SHARE IN EMBER'S DISCOVERY...
SUNTOP!
LOOK WHAT I FOUND!!

BONES!
HERE'S A FUNNY-LOOKING ONE -- SEE?
RRR-RRUFF! YAP!

AND HERE'S MORE OF 'EM, MOTHER ...LOOK!
TRANSFIXED, LEETAH BARELY HEARS HER DAUGHTER...
TH-THIS IS AN ELF'S SKULL! IT HAS BEEN BARE OF FLESH...FOR ONLY A ...FEW YEARS!
SUDDENLY, SUNTOP TINGLES WITH HIS SPECIAL AWARENESS...
MOTHER...! THESE ROCKS WERE MOVED BY MAGIC! I FEEL IT!
MOVED... BY MAGIC...! ONLY ONE ELF I EVER KNEW COULD LIFT OBJECTS BY HIS WILL ALONE!

AS LEETAH TENDERLY REPLACES THE PATHETIC REMAINS IN THEIR SMALL TOMB, THE WOLFRIDERS CANNOT HELP BUT FEEL SOME SYMPATHY -- AND EVEN A LITTLE REGRET.
COME, SUNTOP... EMBER... IT'S TIME TO GO.
COMPELLED BY A SENSE OF URGENCY WHICH HE CANNOT BEGIN TO EXPLAIN, SUNTOP GUIDES THE RESCUE PARTY WITH SINGLE-MINDED PURPOSE!
ALL THROUGH THE NIGHT THE ELFIN BAND TRAVELS AT A STEADY PACE, HUGGING THE CLIFF BASE, NOTING HOW THE SHEER WALL OF ROCK GROWS GRADUALLY MORE JAGGED AND TUMBLED.
AND FINALLY...
THROUGH THERE, MOTHER!
THAT'S WHERE WE HAVE TO GO!
WHEE-EEW! SO THE TUNNEL OF GOLDEN LIGHT WASN'T THE ONLY PASS THROUGH THESE CLIFFS AFTER ALL!

LISTEN EVERYBODY! ECHOES!
OOOOWWWWWOOOOO
OWWWOOOOOOO
OWWOOO

QUIET, CUB! HUMANS COULD BE LURKING ANYWHERE!
ULP OH...

I'VE SEEN SAVAH'S POWERS...AND I BELIEVE IN 'EM...BUT I'D SURE LIKE TO KNOW WHAT THIS "EVIL THING" IS WE'RE SUPPOSED TO SAVE CUTTER FROM!

THE NARROW GORGE WINDS THROUGH THE ROCKS, SLOPING EVER UPWARD...

LEETAH'S HEART IS GRIPPED BY WRENCHING, VOICELESS FEAR, FOR SHE KNOWS THAT VERY SOON SHE MUST FACE THE TERRORS OF THE LEGENDARY GREEN-GROWING-PLACE...

...THE LAND OF HUMANS!

AFTER LONG MOMENTS OF TENSE WAITING, THE "SPIRITS" APPEAR! THEIR LARGE, MYSTERIOUS EYES BURN LIKE COLD FLAME AS THEY ASCEND THE HIGH PLACE.

AGAIN THE HUMANS ARE OVERCOME WITH AWE AS THEY SEE THEIR OLDEST LEGEND COME TO LIFE!

THE CELEBRATION BEGINS. **OLBAR'S** WARRIORS DISPLAY THEIR STRENGTH AND AGILITY IN A WILD DANCE. DRUMS AND RATTLES PROVIDE DRIVING RHYTHMS WHILE HIGH-PITCHED VOICES SING IN PRAISE OF THE BOUNTIFUL FOREST AND THE EVER-FLOWING RIVER.

TO **CUTTER** AND **SKYWISE,** THE HUMANS' RITE IS, IN MANY WAYS, A TRAVESTY OF THE FESTIVITIES ONCE HELD BY THE **SUN FOLK** IN HONOR OF THE WOLFRIDERS' ARRIVAL. THE DANCING IS HEAVY-FOOTED AND AWKWARD COMPARED TO ELFIN DELICACY...THE MUSIC IS DISSONANT TO SENSITIVE POINTED EARS...

AND YET...

FOR ALL THEIR AGE-OLD -- AND JUSTIFIABLE -- RESENTMENT OF HUMANS...THE "TALL ONES" WHO ARE SO STRANGELY DIVERSE IN APPEARANCE AND SO VIOLENTLY UNPREDICTABLE IN TEMPERAMENT --

-- **CUTTER** AND **SKYWISE** OBSERVE THAT A SMILE IS A SMILE AND A TOUCH IS A TOUCH AMONG HUMANS AND ELVES ALIKE.

FOR HIS PART, **OLBAR** CANNOT TEAR HIS EYES AWAY FROM THESE GHOSTLY, PALE-HAIRED BEINGS WHO SEEM BATHED IN THE MOON'S COOL RADIANCE -- EVEN IN BROAD DAYLIGHT...

<THEIR POWER IS ***VERY GREAT!*** IT DRAWS ME TO THEM!>

<BUT WHY?>
<THEY ARE NO BIGGER THAN CHILDREN... AND YET, WHEN I LOOK AT THEM...I AM THE CHILD!>

RUM TATATUM!
RATTLE! RATTLE!
<YOU SEE, THIEF?>
<OLBAR IS SEDUCED BY THE DARK MAGIC OF THE BEAST-EARED ONES!>

<HE WILL BRING EVIL ON US ALL IN HIS WEAKNESS! BUT IF I WERE TO DEAL WITH THESE DEMONS -->
<-- AH! HOW I WOULD MAKE THEM BOW TO ME!>
<THAT CHARM THE WHITE-HAIRED ONE WEARS ABOUT HIS NECK ...IT IS THE SOURCE OF ALL THEIR POWER! I'M SURE OF IT!>

<WITH THAT MAGIC STONE... I COULD WORK WONDERS!>

<GET IT FOR ME, THIEF! STEAL ME THE DEMONS' TALISMAN OF POWER AND I WILL REWARD YOU!>
<HOW?>
<I WILL GIVE YOU BACK THE THINGS YOU WANT MOST-- YOUR PLACE IN THE TRIBE... YOUR WARRIOR'S SPEAR... AND YOUR NAME!>
<MY NAAAAME...! I'D KILL TO REGAIN IT!>
UNAWARE OF THE BONE WOMAN'S PLAN, SKYWISE IS, NEVERTHELESS, READY AND EAGER TO DEPART...
I'VE HAD ENOUGH, CUTTER. THERE'S NOTHING FOR US HERE.
MAYBE YOU'RE RIGHT, FRIEND.
<HUMAN, YOU AND YOUR PEOPLE HAVE DONE THE SPIRITS HONOR -- BUT NOW WE MUST LEAVE!>
<LEAVE?!>
<YES...NONNA AND ADAR HAVE A PROMISE TO FULFILL... ISN'T THAT SO?>
<YES! AND GLADLY!>
<WE WILL SHOW YOU THE GREAT RIVER!>

<HURRY... BEFORE THEY SLIP AWAY INTO THE FOREST!>
<THIS POTION WILL TAKE AWAY YOUR SCENT! THOSE WOLF GUARDS WILL NOT BETRAY YOU! GO! AND BE SUCCESSFUL -- IF YOU VALUE YOUR LIFE!>
RUM—TA TA—TUM TUM
RUM—TA TA—TUM TUM
<HEAR ME, SPIRITS, BEFORE YOU DEPART!>
<ONLY YOU CAN GRANT THE FAVOR I WOULD ASK!>
ANOTHER FAVOR?! IS THERE NO END TO THEM?
<WAIT, I SAY!>
GROWL
GRRR
OLBAR'S IMPETUOUS COMMAND IS INSTANTLY OVERRIDDEN BY TWO MOST PERSUASIVE ARGUMENTS!
RUM—TA TA—TUM TUM
<BEWARE, HUMAN! YOU MUST NOT FOLLOW US!>
<ONLY NONNA AND ADAR HAVE THAT PRIVILEGE!>
RUM—TA TA—TUM TUM
THE DRUMS STILL BEAT... THE SINGING STILL SOARS... DROWNING THE FAINT RUSTLE OF LEAVES...

EEEAAAAAPPA!

<THIEF! YOU CRAZY SCAVENGER DOG!!>

MY HAND!! MY HAAAND!!

<NEXT TIME IT'LL BE SOMETHING MORE *VITAL!*>

<YOU HUMANS HAVE *TOO MANY* FINGERS, ANYWAY!>

CLUTCHING HIS THUMBLESS HAND, THE THIEF FLEES INTO THE WOODS WITH **NIGHTRUNNER** *AND* **STARJUMPER** *SNAPPING AT HIS HEELS.*

YOU ALL RIGHT...?

HE -- HE TRIED TO STEAL THE *LODESTONE!* WHY DIDN'T WE SCENT HIM COMING, *CUTTER?*

I DON'T *KNOW!*

<THAT WORM RIDDEN PICK-FEAST! I SHOULD HAVE KILLED HIM LONG AGO!>
<BUT...WASN'T THAT YOUR BROTHER, MY CHIEF?>
<NO MORE!>
<HE HAS NO NAME!>
<I TOOK IT AWAY FROM HIM!>
ADAR GASPS, WONDERING WHAT CRIME COULD MERIT A PUNISHMENT WORSE THAN DEATH!

<FORGIVE THIS INSULT, GENTLE SPIRITS. DO NOT TAKE REVENGE UPON MY PEOPLE!>
<WE ARE ANGRY, BUT WE WILL FORGIVE -- IF YOU KEEP YOUR PROMISE -->
<-- TO TREAT NONNA AND ADAR WELL.>
<AND REMEMBER, DON'T TRUST THE BONE WOMAN!>
<SHE'S A CROOKED OLD WEASEL OUT FOR HER OWN GOOD!>

THE RIVER THRASHES IN ITS ROCKY BED, RESTLESS AND FOAM-WHITE. ADAR MUST SHOUT TO BE HEARD ABOVE THE ROARING WATER...
<THE VALLEY OF ENDLESS SLEEP LIES THAT WAY, AND FAR BEYOND IT, THE BLUE MOUNTAIN WHERE I FOUND NONNA!>
<THE QUICKEST WAY TO GET TO THE VALLEY IS TO CLIMB DOWN THE CLIFFS WHERE THE DEATH WATER FALLS!>
<IT'S VERY DANGEROUS, BUT I DID IT -- AND I'M NOT EVEN A SPIRIT!>

‹VINES LIKE THESE HELPED ME MAKE MY DESCENT LONG AGO. IF THEY HELD *ME* IT'S CERTAIN THEY'LL HOLD *YOU!*›

‹WHAT A PITY THAT YOU DO NOT HAVE YOUR GREAT *BOND-BIRDS* TO RIDE!›

‹BUT NO MATTER...YOU WILL WALK SAFELY IN THE VALLEY.›

‹IT HOLDS DANGERS ONLY FOR FOOLHARDY *MEN* -- NOT FOR *BIRD SPIRITS!*›

CUTTER NODS, WISHING HIS CONTINUED DECEPTION OF THESE KIND AND TRUSTING HUMANS WAS NOT NECESSARY.

‹*ADAR'S* TRIBE HAS ACCEPTED ME AS YOU COMMANDED.›

‹I AM *HAPPY!*›

‹BUT... YOU LOOK *SAD!*›

‹OH... IT IS JUST THAT YOU ARE BOTH SO *FAIR,* LIKE THE *DAWN!* BESIDE YOU, WE ARE NO BETTER THAN COARSE AND CLUMSY *TOADS!*›

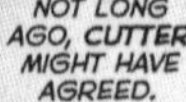

NOT LONG AGO, *CUTTER* MIGHT HAVE AGREED.

BUT NOW...

‹NO! YOU ARE THE FIRST HUMANS TO TOUCH US WITH LOVE IN-STEAD OF HATE!›
‹WE ARE DIFFERENT, BUT I SEE NO UGLINESS IN YOU!›

WHILE THE ELVES TAKE THEIR LEAVE OF NONNA AND ADAR, THE BONE WOMAN TENDS THE THIEF'S WOUND IN A SECRET MEETING PLACE.
<KEEP CHEWING THAT WACKROOT!>
<IT WILL TAKE AWAY THE PAIN AND MAKE YOU FEEL STRONG!>

<I TELL YOU, THIEF, EACH BONE I WEAR HAS A MEMORY...AND THE OLDEST OF THEM WHISPERS TO ME "BEWARE...THE BEAST-EARED ONES WILL BE YOUR DOWNFALL!">

<THEY HAVE ALREADY TURNED OLBAR AGAINST ME!>

<VERY WELL THEN. IF OLBAR REFUSES MY COUNSEL -- LET HIM BE CHIEF NO MORE!>

<YOU WILL TAKE HIS PLACE IF YOU GET ME THE DEMONS' CHARM OF POWER!>
<DO NOT FAIL THIS TIME OR WE ARE BOTH DEAD!>

<AND WHAT OF THE ONE WHO COST ME A THUMB?>
<KILL HIM!>
<KILL THEM BOTH IF THEY CAN BE KILLED! WHAT NEED WE FEAR THEIR FELLOW SPIRITS' REVENGE -->
<-- WHEN I CONTROL THE DARK MAGIC STONE!>

<YOU WILL MAKE ME CHIEF IN OLBAR'S PLACE -->
<SWEAR IT!!>
GAG CHOKE <O-ON MY OATH!>

ONCE AGAIN THE CRAFTY BONE WOMAN ANNOINTS THE THIEF WITH HER SCENT-STEALING POTION...
<GO!>
<YOU WILL FIND THE DEMONS SOMEWHERE NEAR THE RIVER!>
<AYE! AND WHEN I'VE DESTROYED THEM, YOU CROAKING FROG -->
<-- I MAY JUST KEEP THE MAGIC STONE FOR MYSELF!>

THE RAGING RAPIDS PLUNGE ABRUPTLY OVER A SHEER PRECIPICE --
DEATH-WATER!
I CAN SEE, NOW, WHY THE HUMANS CHOSE THAT NAME!
-- CRASHING ONTO A BED OF JAGGED ROCK --
-- FAR, FAR BELOW!
IT'S QUITE A CLIMB!
YOU'D BETTER NOT LOOK DOWN WHILE WE'RE DOING IT, CUTTER!
THINK I'D PLANNED TO?
SAVE YOUR VOICE AND SEND! IT'S EASIER!

WHAT ABOUT NIGHTRUNNER AND STARJUMPER?
THEY CAN'T FOLLOW US THIS WAY!
MAYBE THEY COULD TAKE A LONGER WAY AROUND ...MEET US LATER IN THE VALLEY?
NIGHTRUNNER...?
GRRR...
SNAP!
.......!
NIGHTRUNNER...!
WHY?!

SLOWLY, THE SAD TRUTH DAWNS...

HE'S... ALL WORN OUT, **SKYWISE.** **NIGHTRUNNER** WON'T BE TRAVELING WITH US ANY MORE!

WHINE!

MY FIRST WOLF!

THESE OLD BONES ACHE, DON'T THEY? AND YOUR COAT IS DULL AND DRY... EYES ARE BAD...

OH, **NIGHTRUNNER!**

THE LANGUAGE OF TOUCH AND SCENT SPEAKS A MORE MEANINGFUL FAREWELL THAN SENDING POSSIBLY COULD. **NIGHTRUNNER** DOES NOT KNOW THAT HE MAY NEVER SEE HIS ELF-FRIEND AGAIN, FOR HIS THOUGHTS NEVER FLY BETOND THE NEEDS OF THE MOMENT.

THE OLD WOLF KNOWS ONLY THAT HE IS TIRED, AND THAT THE NEARBY FOREST BECKONS HIM TO REST IN ITS COOL AND SHADOWY DEPTHS.

NIGHTRUNNER'S GOING AWAY. YOU'LL MISS HIM, WON'T YOU, STARJUMPER -- AS MUCH AS I'D MISS CUTTER...IF...
GO ON... I UNDERSTAND!
WHUF!
THEY -- THEY'RE BOTH GOING!
YES... STARJUMPER'S STILL STRONG. HE CAN LOOK AFTER NIGHTRUNNER...HUNT FOR HIM UNTIL --
-- YES.
IT IS "THE WAY," AN ORDER OF THINGS TO BE ACCEPTED WITH SADNESS -- BUT NOT WITH DESPAIR -- FOR IT IS A GOOD WAY, UNCHANGED SINCE THE FIRST BONDING OF WOLF AND ELF.

<LUCK IS WITH ME!>
<THE BEASTS WILL NOT BE HERE TO *PROTECT* THEIR DEMON MASTERS!>

<I MUST BE *SWIFT!*>
<THE DEMONS MAKE READY TO DESCEND THE CLIFFS!>

SHHUSSHHHRROOAARRRR
THERE NOW! THIS'D HOLD *EIGHT* OF US EASILY!
GOOD! LET'S GET GOING! WE'RE STILL TOO NEAR THE HUMANS TO SUIT ME!

<NOW, FROST-HAIRED ONE -->
<-- YOU WILL *PAY* FOR MAIMING MY HAND!>

I CAN SEE THE BLUE MOUNTAIN! SOMETHING TELLS ME OUR QUEST WILL SOON BE DONE!

<A DEADLY STONE FOR A DEMON -- AND SO A MAGIC STONE FOR ME!>
WHIT! WHIT! WHIT! WHIT!
THE SLING WHIRLS -- AND AT THE SAME TIME, ON THE FAR SIDE OF THE VALLEY OF ENDLESS SLEEP...
DON'T WORRY, LITTLE CUB. WE'LL SOON BE ON OUR WAY!
NO!
THIS ISN'T THE RIGHT PLACE! WE CAN'T STAY HERE! IT'S DANGEROUS!
GENTLY, SUNTOP... BE CALM!
WE'RE ALL TIRED. WE NEED TO REST!
AND CHOP-LICKER'S HUNGRY! HE NEEDS MEAT!

LOOK AT THE SIZE OF THAT BIRD, STRONGBOW!
THERE'S ENOUGH MEAT ON 'IM TO FEED US ALL! THINK YOU CAN GET 'IM?
SOB SOB
IS HE ALL RIGHT, LEETAH?
HE IS EXHAUSTED, MOONSHADE! SAVAH'S WARNING IS A TERRIBLE BURDEN FOR ONE SO YOUNG!
WELL, A FULL BELLY OUGHT TO CHEER HIM UP!
LOOK, SUNTOP! STRONGBOW WILL GET US OUR EVENING MEAL --
-- THEN WE CAN CONTINUE TO SEARCH FOR YOUR FATHER!
"THINK YOU CAN GET 'IM?" HUH!
NO!
HE MUSTN'T KILL THAT BIRD!

TWO MISSLES FLY WITH DEADLY ACCURACY --
THUNNG!
WHISH!
-- STREAK TOWARD THEIR UNWITTING TARGETS --
-- AND UNERRINGLY STRIKE HOME!
UNH!!
WHOKK!

WHA--?!
SKYWISE!
⟨FOOLISH DEMON! LOOK TO YOUR OWN LIFE!⟩
THE THIEF!
LIGHTNING SWIFT, CUTTER WHIRLS AND DRAWS HIS SWORD --
-- JUST AS THE STONE HURTLES FULL FORCE AT HIS UNPROTECTED HEAD!
SHOK!
AAGH!

GREEDILY THE THIEF LUNGES TOWARD SKYWISE'S STILL FORM!
<AWAY, DEMON! THE MAGIC STONE IS MINE!>
GROWLING LIKE AN ANGRY WOLF, CUTTER GROPES WITH HIS UNINJURED HAND FOR HIS FALLEN WEAPON.
AS THOUGH WEIGHTLESS, THE AGILE ELF CHIEFTAIN LEAPS CLEAR OF THE HUMAN'S FLAILING CLUB!
HAARG!!

BUT AS CUTTER SLASHES IN TURN....
<HA HA! THE BONE WOMAN'S MEDICINE GIVES ME SPEED TO MATCH YOURS, DEMON! SOON I WILL HAVE ALL YOUR POWERS, AND YOU WILL LIE AS STILL AS YOUR COMPANION!>
ZWISSHHH!
THUMP!
<YOU LIKE TO KILL, DO YOU, HUMAN?>
SO DO I, WHEN I MUST!>
YOU ARE MEAT TO BE WASTED!
<YOUR BLOOD WILL FALL ON BARE ROCK -->
<-- AND NOURISH NOTHING!>

TOWERING ABOVE HIS DIMINUTIVE FOE, THE **THIEF** ROARS WITH INCREDULOUS MIRTH!

‹ ***YOU?!*** YOU WOULD **STICK ME** WITH YOUR SINGLE SPINE, LITTLE ***QUILL-PIG?*** ›
HAH HAHAHA HAHA HAHA!
‹ I COULD ***WEAR*** YOU IN PLACE OF MY LOST ***THUMB!*** ›

‹ ARE ***THESE*** THE MIGHTY SPIRITS I WAS TAUGHT IN MY YOUTH TO ***FEAR?*** ›
‹ THE LEGENDS ***LIE!!*** ›
BAH!
‹ YOU ***CAN DIE!*** ›
‹ YOU HAVE ***BLOOD,*** AND IT FLOWS AS RED AS ***ANY*** BEAST'S! ›

‹ BEFORE THIS DAY IS DONE, I SHALL BE THE ***GREATEST CHIEFTAIN OF ALL!!*** ›
‹ AND I SHALL HAVE A ***NEW*** NAME! ›

‹ THEY WILL CALL ME -- ›
‹ -- **SPIRIT SLAYER!** ›

HUUUUH..!
<Y-YOU...!>
<YOU'VE KILLED ME!>
<YOU MADE IT *EASY* FOR ME, HUMAN!>

CUTTER WATCHES IMPASSIVELY AS THE DYING MAN STAGGERS BACK -- TOWARD THE LEDGE!
OOHHH...

THE THIEF FALLS!

BUT HIS ARMS FLY OUT... HIS FINGERS CLUTCH REFLEX-IVELY --

-- AND HE IS LEFT HANGING BETWEEN LIFE AND DEATH UPON THE COLD LEDGE OF...

<STONE!>

<MUST HAVE... MAGIC STONE!>

NO! LET GO!!
IT'S MINE!!

SKYWISE!

NO!
FOR A TERRIBLE MOMENT, HUMAN AND ELF SHARE ONE FEAR -- ONE FATE --

-- AND THEN ONE CHANCE FOR LIFE!
UNH!

THE MAN, ALREADY DEAD, STRIKES THE WATER AND VANISHES! BUT SKYWISE, VERY MUCH ALIVE, FEELS THE WITHERED ROOT GIVING WAY EVEN UNDER HIS SLIGHT WEIGHT!

QUICK! GRAB THE VINE!!
I-I CAN'T!
MY ARM WON'T WORK!

HANG ON... HANG ON, FRIEND!

HIGH ONES HELP ME --

A SICK, DIZZY FEELING SWEEPS OVER CUTTER AS HIS FEAR OF HEIGHTS WELLS WITHIN HIM!

-- I'M COMING!
HURRY!

DON'T MOVE! I'LL GET YOU!
KRIK! KRAK!
SHOCK AND PAIN BEGIN TO CONQUER SKYWISE!

WAKE UP!!
YOU'VE GOT TO STAY AWAKE!
UNNHH...
THAT'S IT... HOLD ON TO ME!
I'LL PULL US BOTH UP!
NO GOOD!
HE CAN'T DO IT!
GOT TO USE ONE ARM TO KEEP HIM FROM SLIPPING OFF MY BACK -- BUT HOW CAN I MOVE THIS WAY?!
<CURSE YOU, HUMANS!!>
<CURSE EVERY LAST ONE OF YOUR MURDERING SOULS!>
<AND A CURSE ON ME TOO -- FOR TRUSTING ANY OF YOU!!>

WHA--?
THE VINE!
IT'S *MOVING!*

SOMEONE'S PULLING US UP!

IS IT *ADAR?*
I *PRAY* IT IS...
WE'RE IN NO SHAPE TO TAKE ON ANOTHER *THIEF!*

<WELL NOW! IS *OLBAR* INCLUDED IN YOUR CURSE, LITTLE SPIRIT?>
<IF SO, WHAT A *PITY!*>
<AFTER ALL, IT IS MY "CURSED" HAND THAT AIDS YOU NOW!>

<HOW LUCKY YOU ARE THAT I FOUND THE COURAGE TO FOLLOW YOU AGAINST YOUR COMMAND!>
<BUT WAIT!>

<I THINK I'LL JUST LET YOU DANGLE THERE A BIT...>

THE GIANT HUMAN'S INTENT IS UNGUESSABLE...
<WHY DON'T YOU FLY TO SAVE YOURSELVES, BIRD SPIRITS?>

<CAN IT BE THAT YOU HAVE NO REAL POWERS?>
<THAT -- PERHAPS -- YOU ARE NOT SPIRITS AFTER ALL?>

<IF I CUT THIS VINE I THINK, PERHAPS, YOU WILL FALL AND DROWN -->
MOMENTS PASS, MEASURED BY THE POUNDING OF TWO AGONIZED ELFIN HEARTS...
<-- BUT THEN, YOU COULD NOT ANSWER MY QUESTIONS, COULD YOU?>
PLACING THE ELVES SAFELY ON THE LEDGE, OLBAR STARES AT THEM LONG AND SILENTLY BEFORE HE SPEAKS...
<WHAT ARE YOU? YOU ARE NOT IMMORTAL. YOU FEEL PAIN AND FEAR DEATH AS WE DO. YET YOU LOOK SO STRANGE.>
<THERE ARE ANCIENT TALES OF BEINGS LIKE YOU WHO ONCE RULED THE FOREST.>
<I HAVE ALWAYS FEARED THE SPIRITS...BUT YOU ARE NOT SPIRITS, MEN, CHILDREN OR BEASTS!>
<ANSWER ME TRULY -->
<-- WHAT ARE YOU?>
<NO HUMAN HAS EVER BOTHERED TO ASK!>
<WE HAVE NO ANSWER FOR YOU!>
<WHAT YOU CALL US DOESN'T MATTER. IT ONLY MATTERS THAT HUMANS NEVER NEEDED TO FEAR OR HATE US!>

< I WILL REMEMBER... BUT IF ONLY YOU *WERE* SPIRITS -->
<-- YOU COULD GRANT THE FAVOR I TRIED TO ASK EARLIER.>
<MY DAUGHTER... *SELAH*...>
<"SHE RAN AWAY TO THE *FORBIDDEN GROVE* WITH A YOUTH I DESPISED!">
<"WHEN MY HUNTERS AND I GAVE CHASE --">
<"-- WE WERE DRIVEN FROM THE GROVE BY AN ANGRY SWARM OF THE TINY, WINGED *SPIRITS* WHO DWELL THERE!">

"TO THIS DAY," OLBAR CONTINUES, "I HAVE NOT SEEN MY GIRL-CHILD AGAIN! I HAD HOPED THAT YOU COULD ENTER THE WINGED ONES' DOMAIN SAFELY AND DISCOVER WHAT BECAME OF HER!"

CUTTER REPLIES, AFTER A MOMENT, "MAYBE WE CAN!"

...SO THEN! THERE LIES THE FORBIDDEN GROVE.

NO ONE GOES THERE, FOR IT IS A CURSED PLACE -- AS DEADLY AS A SPIDER'S WEB IS TO A FLY!

CUTTER AND SKYWISE NOD, GAZING INSTEAD BEYOND TO THE DISTANT BLUE PEAKS WHICH ARE THEIR ULTIMATE GOAL.

LATER...
NONNA'S RIGHT!
WITH BONES AS FRAGILE AS THOSE --
-- YOU MUST BE RELATED TO BIRDS!

FARE WELL, THEN, LITTLE BIRD BONES --

OLBAR HAS TOUCHES A "SPIRIT" -- AND HE FEELS HIS FEARS MELT AWAY.

SKYWISE HAS BEEN TOUCHED BY A HUMAN --

-- AND HE HAS SURVIVED THE EXPERIENCE!

-- PERHAPS SOON I WILL HAVE A DAUGHTER AGAIN...

THERE IS ONE FINAL FAREWELL --
OOOOOOWWWWWOOOOOOOOO!
WWWOOOOOOOOOO
-- ANSWERED ONE FINAL TIME.
THEN...
THERE IT IS, SKYWISE. THE REST OF OUR JOURNEY OUGHT TO BE AS SOFT --
"-- AS MOONSHADE'S FINEST LEATHER!"

THE VALLEY OF ENDLESS SLEEP IS A PLACE OF DEEP GREEN SILENCES...
ONLY THOSE WHO WALK WITHOUT BREAKING THE SILENCE ARE WELCOME HERE.

WE'RE TWO NIGHTS CLOSER TO BLUE MOUNTAIN, BUT THE NEARER WE GET, THE LESS CUTTER SEEMS TO CARE!
HE MISSES NIGHTRUNNER... BUT IT'S MORE THAN THAT.

STILL FAR AWAY, OBSCURED BY THE TREES, LIES THE BLUE MOUNTAIN PEAK WHERE THE ELFIN PAIR HOPE TO FIND OTHERS OF THEIR KIND. THOUGH THERE HAS NEVER BEEN MUCH NEED FOR WORDS BETWEEN THEM, SKYWISE KNOWS THAT HIS FRIEND'S HEAVY HEART WANTS CHEERING...
LOOK! THE TWO STARS I GAVE YOU AND LEETAH ON YOUR JOINING NIGHT... THEY'RE RIGHT OVERHEAD!
HMM... THEY SEEM FAR APART.

BUT ALWAYS TO-GETHER!
YES... IT'S GOOD TO KNOW THAT LEETAH AND THE CUBS ARE IN SORROW'S END. SHE WAS WISE NOT TO COME WITH ME ON THIS QUEST.
I SUP-POSE THAT MAKES ME A FOOL!

IF YOU HADN'T GRABBED THAT ROOT WHEN YOU FELL... IF YOU HAD DROWNED IN THE DEATHWATER...
I -- I DON'T KNOW WHAT I...

YOU... WOULD HAVE MARCHED RIGHT UP TO THE BIRD SPIRITS AND ANNOUNCED YOURSELF WITH YOUR SWORD!
LUCKILY I'M STILL HERE TO MAKE APOLOGIES FOR MY CHIEF --
-- WHO STILL HAS A FOUL DIS-POSITION AND THE MANNERS OF A TROLL!

TROLLS... GET *EVEN!*

LIKE SWIFT RABBITS THE ELVES DART THROUGH THE CONCEALING UNDERGROWTH.

THE SILENCE IS BROKEN BY THEIR CARELESS LAUGHTER...

THE FORBIDDEN GROVE
THIS IS THE PLACE THE GIANT HUMAN CHIEF TOLD US ABOUT, ISN'T IT?
THE *FORBIDDEN GROVE!*
WHAT DID HE SAY? "AS *DEADLY* AS A *SPIDER'S WEB IS TO A FLY*"?
OLBAR CLAIMED HIS DAUGHTER WENT IN THERE AND NEVER CAME OUT!
I WONDER WHAT REALLY HAPPENED TO *HIM* THAT HE'S SO AFRAID OF THIS WOOD?
WE OWE HIM A FAVOR...WANT TO GO IN AND LOOK FOR THE HUMAN GIRL?
MIGHT AS WELL...
THOUGH IT'S PROBABLY A WASTE OF TIME!
NOW I KNOW WHY THE HUMANS CALL THIS THE VALLEY OF ENDLESS SLEEP. IT'S SO QUIET AND STILL, YOU CAN'T EVEN FEEL THE NIGHT BREEZE!
BUT YOU CAN FEEL THESE STICKY *SPIDER NETS!* THEY'RE ALL OVER!

THE ELVES STEAL THROUGH THE FORBIDDEN GROVE AS SOUNDLESSLY AS ONLY WOLFRIDERS CAN. EVERYWHERE THEY LOOK, STREAMERS OF GOSSAMER WEBBING HANG FROM THE TREES, SHIMMERING IN THE STARLIGHT.

LOOK! COCOONS! TOO MANY OF THEM TO COUNT!

WHAT KIND OF INSECT SPINS THREAD LIKE *THIS?*

NO SPIDER OR CATERPILLAR I EVER HEARD OF...

LET ME GUESS... YOU'RE CURIOUS, AREN'T YOU!

ALL RIGHT... LET'S CUT ONE OPEN AND SEE WHAT IT HOLDS!

TWITTER! CHIRP!

TSIPP!

MEAT EATERS! THEY TRAP LIVE CREATURES IN COCOONS TO KEEP THE BLOOD FRESH!
LOOKS LIKE. BUT WHY IS THERE SO MUCH MEAT HERE -- AND NONE OF IT EATEN?
ALL THE COCOONS ARE PERFECT -- UNBROKEN -- SEE? IT'S WEIRD!
MORE THAN WEIRD!
WHERE ARE THESE WEB WEAVERS? AND WHAT ARE THEY?
SKYWISE, REMEMBER WHAT OLBAR SAID?
HE WAS CHASED AWAY FROM HERE BY "WINGED SPIRITS."
WHAT DO YOU THINK HE MEANT?
SKYW--?
HURTS?
YOU SIT THERE AND REST AWHILE.

I'LL DO A LITTLE MORE EXPLORING.
ALL RIGHT. IT'S PEACEFUL ENOUGH. YOU SHOULDN'T GET INTO TOO MUCH TROUBLE WITHOUT ME.
AND I AM... TIRED.....

MOMENTS LATER...

TANNER'S NEEDLES!

WHAT COULD BE INSIDE *THIS* ONE? IT'S SO *BIG!*

YUGH!

THIS STUFF IS STICKIER THAN OLD *HONEY!*

UH?

HEH HEH HEH! YOU'RE A FRIENDLY LITTLE ONE! AND WELL FED, TOO!
YOUR PACK CAN'T HAVE ABANDONED YOU TOO LONG AGO!

NIGHTRUNNER WASN'T MUCH BIGGER THAN YOU WHEN HE AND I BONDED...
CUTTER NUZZLES THE CUB'S SOFT FUR -- AND SUDDENLY...

EMBER!! BY ALL THE CHILDREN OF THE HIGH ONES! THIS CUB HAS MY DAUGHTER'S SCENT ON HIM!!

INSTANTLY THE YOUNG CHIEF WHIRLS AND DASHES BACK TO SKYWISE.
MY NOSE HAS NEVER LIED TO ME BEFORE...BUT THIS IS TOO CRAZY TO BELIEVE!

UNDOUBTEDLY **SKYWISE** WOULD SAY THE SAME OF HIS OWN STRANGE PREDICAMENT --

-- IF HE WERE AWAKE!

NO NO NO NO!! STILLQUIET HIGHTHING GOT FUNNY ARM! SEE?

ALL BROKE!

CAN'T PUT IN WRAPSTUFF.

IS NOT GOOD ALL OVER!

IS GOOD ENOUGH! PETALWING KNOWS! PETALWING SAY SO!

THIS STILLQUIET HIGHTHING VERY IMPORTANT! GOES WITH OTHER ONES! HUSHUP NOW AND MAKE WRAPSTUFF!
WE DO!
GRUMBLE WE DO!
WE DO!

EEP!

WHAT ARE YOU DOING TO HIM?! YOU GREEDY LITTLE --
EEEEEE!
ZWIISSHH!
MMM... MNHUH?
ZWAAASSHH!
GET OUT OF HERE!!
?!

NOISYBAD HIGHTHING!!

PLUZHT!

YAP! YARF!

CUTTER?

HEE HEE!
WE SCRATCH!
WE STING!
WE CHASE AWAY
BAD HIGHTHING!
OW!
STOP
IT --
-- OR I'LL
PULL THIS ONE'S
WINGS OFF!
THE THREAT WORKS!
OOOHH -- POOR
PETALWING!
DON'T
PULL!
DON'T
PULL!
BEESWEETS AND
JUICEBERRIES WE
FETCH FOR YOU!
NIIIICE
HIGHTHING!
TELL YOUR
FRIENDS TO LEAVE US
ALONE AND -- MAYBE -- YOU
CAN KEEP YOUR WINGS!
GO WAY!
GO WAY!
PETAL-
WING
SAY SO!
SO THESE
ARE THE
COCOON
SPINNERS!
WHURF?
RELUCTANTLY,
THE FLITTERING,
MULTI-COLORED
BEINGS ABANDON
THEIR CAPTURED
COMPANION,
HIDING THEMSELVES
AMONG THE
TREES.

-KOFF- WELL, NOW YOU KNOW WHO MUCKED UP THE WOODS WITH ALL THIS GOO!
YES...BUT IT LOOKS LIKE YOU'VE BROUGHT ME ANOTHER MYSTERY! WHERE'D YOU FIND THE CUB?
THAT DOESN'T MATTER. TAKE A WHIFF OF HIS FUR --
-- AND TELL ME IF I'M CRAZY!
-SNIF-
EMBER?!
IT'S TRUE!
YOU! PETALWING! TELL WHAT YOU KNOW ABOUT THIS CUB!
AND NO TRICKS!
NO TRICKS! NO TRICKS!
FUR-SOFT YAP-THING --
-- COME TWO DARKS AGO!

COME WITH OTHER HIGHTHINGS --
-- TWO LITTLE -- ONE BIG!
"OTHERS"... LIKE ME? WHERE? WHERE ARE THEY?
WON'T TELL!
YAACHH!
PLOOTZ!

HEE HEE HEE!

THAT LITTLE BUG TALKS A LOT BUT DOESN'T SAY MUCH, EH, CUTTER?
...CUTTER?

HE RUNS, AS THOUGH MADCOIL WERE ONCE MORE AT HIS HEELS!

HEY!!

SKYWISE CAN BARELY KEEP UP WITH HIS CHIEF, WHO SEEMS SUDDENLY POSSESSED!

HE'S GONE OUT OF HIS *HEAD!*
A *WALL OF FIRE* WOULDN'T STOP HIM NOW...
"...BUT WHERE IS HE GOING?"
CUTTER HAS NEITHER TIME NOR PATIENCE TO EXPLAIN HIS ACTIONS.
ABRUPTLY HE STOPS...TENSES... TESTS HIS SURROUNDINGS WITH EVERY KEEN ELFIN SENSE AT HIS COMMAND.
HE'S *SENDING!*
DOES HE *BELIEVE PETALWING'S* BABBLING?!

FAINTLY, FROM THE DARKNESS AHEAD COMES A FALTERING, UNSKILLED RESPONSE!
IT IS ENOUGH!

NO NO NO!!
DON'T CUT WRAP-STUFF!

BAD HIGHTHING!!
GO AWAY, BUG!

THE GRIM, SWORD SHARP TONE OF CUTTER'S COMMAND SILENCES THE PUGNACIOUS SPRITE.
WITH THE MOST DELICATE CARE HE SLICES THROUGH THE GLOSSY THREADS...

STRAND BY STRAND, NEW MOON UNCOVERS THAT WHICH CUTTER SUSPECTED --

-- BUT HARDLY DARED HOPE HE WOULD SEE!

...T-TAM...?

OH, TAM!!

EVEN AS SHE CRIES ALOUD HER LIFEMATE'S SECRET SOUL NAME, LEETAH SEES SKYWISE AND...
OH BELOVED! FORGIVE ME!
IT'S ALL RIGHT, LEETAH...
SKYWISE KNOWS MY SOUL NAME!
HE HAS ALWAYS KNOWN IT!
OF COURSE! BROTHERS IN ALL BUT BLOOD! I SHOULD HAVE GUESSED!
BUT YOUR ARM! WHAT HAPPENED?
TROLL WARTS AND LIZARD SKINS, LEETAH! MY ARM CAN WAIT!
WHAT ARE YOU DOING HERE?!!

THE SINGLE, SIMPLE QUESTION RELEASES A **FLOOD** OF EXCITED AND CONFUSED ANSWERS -- IT IS THE SWEETEST MUSIC **CUTTER** HAS EVER HEARD!

THE CHATTER OF DEARLY-LOVED VOICES...THE SCENT AND FEEL OF HIS FAMILY'S NEARNESS...THE SIGHT OF WIDE-EYED, FLUSHED FACES -- AND THE BURDEN OF A PERILOUS JOURNEY DISSOLVES IN PEALS OF JOYOUS LAUGHTER!

THOUGH **LEETAH** AND THE TWINS ARE STILL LEARNING THE ART OF SENDING, **CUTTER** AND **SKYWISE** ARE ABLE TO HELP THEM CALL FORTH IMAGES OF THEIR RECENT ORDEAL...

THE WOLFRIDERS CAME OUT OF THE DESERT AND CAMPED BY THE BANKS OF A NARROW RIVER THAT SLICED THROUGH THE VALLEY.
A HUGE, SOARING BIRD, WITH A WINGSPAN AS WIDE AS SIX WOLVES SET NOSE TO TAIL, PROVIDED UNEXPECTED BOUNTY FOR THE MEAT-HUNGRY ELVES.
NO ONE COULD UNDERSTAND WHY SUNTOP BEGGED STRONGBOW NOT TO SHOOT THE CREATURE DOWN.
AS WOLVES AND RIDERS FEASTED ON THE WARM, PALE MEAT, SCOUTER SUDDENLY JUMPED UP AND POINTED TOWARD SUN-GOES-DOWN.
FROM BEHIND A CURTAIN OF FLAME-COLORED CLOUD, A FLIGHT OF SEVEN MAJESTIC BIRDS -- MUCH LARGER THAN THE SLAIN ONE -- CAME GLIDING TOWARD THE TRAVELERS.
IT WAS AN AWESOME SIGHT, BUT NOT ONE TO INSPIRE FEAR --
-- UNTIL IT WAS TOO LATE!
THE GIGANTIC BIRDS SUDDENLY SWOOPED DOWN UPON THE WOLFRIDERS WITH CLAWS EXTENDED FOR THE ATTACK!

IN MOMENTS STRONGBOW HAD FIRED HIS LAST ARROW!
THE SLENDER SHAFTS THAT HAD KILLED THE SMALLER BIRD COULD NOT PIERCE THESE THICK HIDED MONSTERS...
JUST AS PIKE'S FORCE-FULLY THROWN SPEAR --
-- REBOUNDED AND CLATTERED USELESSLY TO THE GROUND!
IN PANIC, CUTTER'S SON FLED!
SUNTOP!
BROTHER!
IT WAS NOT AN ACT OF COWARDICE, BUT ONE OF DESPERATE DEVOTION!
I HAVE TO FIND FATHER!
I HAVE TO!!
WAIT FOR ME!!
SUNTOP! EMBER!
COME DOWN!!
IT ISN'T SAFE FOR YOU UP THERE!
GASP TOO LATE!
HIDE, MY LITTLE ONES!
HIDE DEEP IN THE BASKET!
SNORT!
GREAT SUN, PROTECT US!

BAWLING ITS TERROR, LEETAH'S ZWOOT BOLTED AWAY FROM THE SWOOPING BLACK SHADOW. THE EMBATTLED WOLFRIDERS WERE SOON LEFT FAR BEHIND.
LEETAH CLUNG TO THE HARNESS, HER MIND EMPTY OF ALL THOUGHT SAVE ONE --
-- NO MATTER WHAT HAPPENED, SHE MUST NOT LOSE HER CHILDREN!
THE DULL-WITTED BEAST GALLOPED FOR WHAT SEEMED LIKE AN ETERNITY!
MORE THAN ONCE LEETAH'S STRENGTH NEARLY GAVE OUT!
SHE WAS DRAGGED, HALF-CONSCIOUS, INTO THE TWILIGHT GLOOM OF A DENSE WOOD...

...THE GREEN GROWING PLACE!
IT WAS MORE MYSTERIOUS AND FRIGHTENING THAN THE SUN VILLAGE'S SHELTERED HEALER HAD EVER IMAGINED!
SUNTOP QUICKLY TOOK THE LEAD.
IT'S GOING TO BE ALL RIGHT, MOTHER!
THIS IS THE PLACE SAVAH TOLD ME TO LOOK FOR!
I KNOW WE'LL FIND FATHER SOON!
BUT "SOON" WAS LONG IN COMING...
NIGHT GREW HEAVY AND DEEP AS THE LITTLE SEARCH PARTY WOVE ITS WAY THROUGH THE THICKET.
AT LAST EVEN SUNTOP HAD TO ADMIT THAT HE HAD REACHED THE LIMIT OF THE GUIDANCE IMPARTED TO HIM BY SAVAH.
THEY WERE LOST...LOST AND DESPERATELY TIRED.
EVEN EMBER WAS TOO WEARY TO CARE --
-- WHEN LITTLE CHOPLICKER WANDERED OFF TO CHASE WHAT HE THOUGHT WAS A BUTTERFLY...

THE STRING OF IMAGES UNWINDS TO ITS END, BUT QUESTIONS REMAIN!
BUT WHY DID YOU COME? WHY DID YOU RISK SO MUCH TO FIND ME?
IT'S SUNTOP! SAVAH PUT A MESSAGE FOR YOU INSIDE HIS HEAD!
WHAT? I - I DON'T UNDERSTAND...
SAVAH "WENT OUT" OF HER BODY TO HELP YOU, FATHER.
SHE FOUND SOME-THING BAD...SOME-THING YOU MUSTN'T GO NEAR!
I "WENT OUT" TO SEE HER AND SHE TOLD ME TO WARN YOU!
BUT WE CAME ALL THIS WAY AND NOW... I - I DON'T KNOW HOW TO DO WHAT SHE TOLD ME.
...I DON'T KNOW HOW!

THAT PEACE AND QUIET SECLUSION WILL HELP THE CHILD CONCENTRATE.
YOU ARE MY SON. I TRUST YOU!
THANK YOU, LEETAH!
LATER...
HA HAH! MY ARM'S AS GOOD AS NEW! WATCH THIS!
WOOP!
UNDER AND OVER --
-- JUST LIKE A LONG-TAILED TREE-WEE!
WHEE! THAT'S FUN! I LIKE THE WOODS!
TEACH ME HOW TO BE A TREE-WALKER, SKYWISE! I WANT TO DO IT, TOO!

YOU WILL, EMBER! THERE'S MUCH FOR YOU TO LEARN HERE!
FATHER! WHAT DID SUNTOP TELL YOU?
IT...CAN'T BE EXPLAINED IN WORDS. SAVAH WAS RIGHT -- THERE IS A DANGER -- AND IT HAS TO DO WITH THE BLUE MOUNTAIN! BUT THE PICTURES AND FEELINGS IN HER WARNINGS ARE NOT VERY CLEAR.
SUNTOP AND I HAVE TO TRY AGAIN, LATER, TO MAKE SENSE OF IT ALL.
RIGHT NOW WE'VE GOT TO GO FIND OUT WHAT HAPPENED TO THE WOLFRIDERS!
THE QUEST MEANS NOTHING IF THEY'VE COME TO HARM!
HIGHTHINGS GOING AWAY!
SO? IS GOOD!
HIGHTHINGS WON'T CUT UP MORE WRAPSTUFF!
BUT PETALWING REMEMBERS BELONGING-TIME!
PETALWING REMEMBERS!!

TTTHHIIPP!
OH!
IS IT A BUTTERFLY?
SOFT-PRETTY HIGH-THINGS
PETALWING GO WITH YOU!
THINK SO?
NOOOOO! NO! NO! PETALWING WANT TO STAAAAY!
LET GO, BUG! YOU'RE NOT WELCOME!
GASP IT CAN SPEAK!
OOO! WHAT IS IT?
CAN I SEE?
YAP! YAP!
WHAT MAKES YOU THINK WE'D WANT YOU AROUND US, PEST? YOU AND YOUR WINGED FRIENDS TRAPPED MY FAMILY IN YOUR WEBS! AND YOU'D DO IT AGAIN IF YOU HAD THE CHANCE!
NO! NO!
BAD HIGHTHING!

THAT'S WHERE YOU BELONG!
WELL! SO MUCH FOR THE EVIL SPIRITS OF THE FORBIDDEN GROVE!
AWW...
SKRISH!
YEEEEEP!!
WHEN WE COME OUT OF THIS WOOD, LEETAH, CAN YOU GUIDE US TO THE PLACE WHERE YOU WERE ATTACKED?
I WILL TRY.
THOSE GIANT BIRDS AND WARNING ALL FIT WITH WHAT SKYWISE AND I LEARNED ABOUT THE "BIRD SPIRITS"!

IT IS SADLY IRONIC, BELOVED...THE WOLF-RIDERS CAME ALONG TO PROTECT THE TWINS AND ME DURING OUR SEARCH FOR YOU. NOW OUR FAMILY IS REUNITED --
-- BUT NIGHT-FALL! REDLANCE! PIKE! AND ALL THE OTHERS --
-- WHERE ARE THEY?!
CUTTER'S ASSURED TONE BELIES HIS CONCERN. BUT FORTUNATELY, A FOREVER BUSY WOLF CUB'S CAREFREE PRESENCE --
WE'LL FIND THEM! WE'LL TRACK THEM 'TIL WE FIND THEM!
-- HELPS TO LIGHTEN THE MOOD!
SO THIS IS CHOPLICKER, EH? SKYWISE, LOOK AT THE SIZE OF HIS PAWS!
HE'S GOING TO BE HUGE!
HE'LL BE EVEN BIGGER THAN NIGHT-RUNNER WAS -- I-I MEAN IS!
EMBER SEES THE WISTFUL LOOK IN CUTTER'S EYES...
WE'LL SEE NIGHTRUNNER AND STARJUMPER AGAIN, WON'T WE, FATHER?
MAYBE...BUT ANYTHING CAN HAPPEN IN THE WOODS! YOU HAVE TO BE READY FOR IT!

I'M READY NOW!
AYOOOAH!!
EMBER IS A WOLFRIDER THROUGH AND THROUGH!
BUT I WONDER...
WILL SUNTOP AND I EVER FEEL AT HOME IN TAM'S WORLD?
WHEEE!
LOOK AT ME!

THE THOUGHT CONTINUES TO TROUBLE LEETAH AS HER FAMILY NEARS THE EDGE OF THE MYSTERIOUS GROVE...
WHERE ARE MOTHER AND FATHER GOING, SKYWISE?
TO BE BY THEMSELVES FOR A WHILE.
TURN AROUND AND PAY ATTENTION! WHATEVER JUMPS OUT OF HERE IS FOOD, BUT YOU'LL HAVE TO CATCH IT!
TOGETHER FOR THE FIRST TIME IN MORE THAN FOUR MOONS, CUTTER AND LEETAH WALK AND TALK QUIETLY. HE TELLS HER OF ALL HIS ADVENTURES. SHE TELLS HIM OF HER UNEASE IN THIS PLACE OF DAMPS AND DECAYS...AND OVERWHELMING LIFE IN EVERY CONCEIVABLE FORM.
THEN, BY MEREST CHANCE, THEY COME UPON A SCENE OF INDESCRIBABLE BEAUTY! WHEN LEETAH IS FINALLY ABLE TO SPEAK, HER VOICE TREMBLES WITH EMOTION...
TAM...? HAVE THE STARS COME DOWN FROM THE SKY TO DANCE ABOVE THE WATER?
THOSE ARE FIREFLIES! SKYWISE LIKES TO CALL THEM "LITTLE STAR COUSINS!"

THIS IS THEIR DANCE OF JOINING.
I - I HAVE NEVER SEEN ANYTHING SO...
OHH...
THE WOOD ISN'T THE DEADLY PLACE YOUR TRIBE'S LEGENDS HAVE MADE IT OUT TO BE, LEETAH. BUT YOU HAVE TO MOVE AND BREATHE AND THINK WITH THE FOREST TO LIVE IN IT!
YOU HAVE TO BECOME A WOLF-RIDER!
HOW? I AM A SUN VILLAGER. HOW CAN I CHANGE?
WELL...FIRST --
-- YOU'LL HAVE TO GET RID OF ALL THIS JINGLING JEWELRY! A WOLFRIDER'S STEPS ARE ALWAYS SILENT...SECRET!
YES...
BUT IF MY JEWELRY MUST GO BECAUSE IT IS TOO NOISY --
-- THEN IT SEEMS TO ME, BELOVED --
-- THAT THIS COAT OF MINE, WHICH RUSTLES SO LOUDLY, MUST GO TOO!

TAM...
I HAVE MISSED YOU!

*!!G!!
PETALWING!
WHAT ARE THESE TINY TALKING CREATURES? THEY SEEM TO SPIN THEIR WEBS FOR NO REASON?
GRUMBLE GROWL

PETALWING GOT REASON!
WRAPSTUFF KEEP SOFTPRETTY HIGHTHINGS SAFE AND SOUND!
PETALWING GO WITH! TAKE GOOD CARE OF HIGHTHINGS!

THAT'S SOME JOKE, BUG!
WHAT ARE YOU GOOD FOR, ANYWAY?

ALL YOU DO IS SPIT GOO ON EVERYTHING! LOOK WHAT YOU'VE DONE TO THIS WOOD!
IT ISN'T FIT TO LIVE IN!

YOU THINK ANYTHING THAT FALLS ASLEEP HERE IS FAIR GAME FOR Y-- !
GASP!

THIS BIGGEST WRAPSTUFF WE EVER DO!
BIGTHINGS BEEN STILL-QUIET HERE LONG TIME!
IS PRETTY? IS PRETTY!
TAM! SOMETHING'S INSIDE THAT ENORMOUS COCOON!
WHAT COULD IT BE?

CONSIDERING HOW I FOUND YOU AND OUR CUBS --
-- I CAN GUESS!
WAIT HERE!
CUTTER'S SLIGHT FORM BARELY STIRS THE GLISTENING, LUMPISH MASS AS HE CRAWLS ONTO IT!
"CUTTER!" HUNH! NEVER THOUGHT I'D LIVE UP TO MY TRIBE NAME THIS WAY!
THAT HUMAN CHIEF, OLBAR, SURE HAS TROUBLE KEEPING HIS FAMILY TOGETHER!
PETALWING! QUIT SEALING UP EVERY CUT I MAKE!
I KNOW WHAT I'M DOING!

AND WHEN THE WORK IS DONE...
SKRASH!!

NOW BE A *WOLFRIDER, LEETAH!* WATCH AND LISTEN AND BE SILENT!

LEETAH SHIVERS WITH DREAD AS TWO LARGE, DARK-SKINNED CREATURES SLOWLY WAKEN AND WORK THEIR WAY FREE OF THE STICKY SHROUD.

...*HUMANS?!*

YAWN *M-MALAK?*

WE HAVE SLEPT BUT *LITTLE,* I THINK...

IT IS NOT YET *DAWN!*

KOFF KOFF

SUSPENDED IN A DREAMLESS SLUMBER WITHIN THE COCOON, THE YOUNG HUMANS DO NOT KNOW THAT THEIR "LITTLE SLEEP" BEGAN MORE THAN A YEAR AGO!

THEY ARE NOT WITHOUT GRACE, THIS TALL, HEALTHY DAUGHTER OF OLBAR AND HER OUTCAST LOVER. HORRIFIED AT FIRST, AND THEN FASCINATED, LEETAH CANNOT CONTAIN HER AMAZEMENT.
I...ALWAYS BELIEVED THAT HUMANS WERE MONSTERS!
SO DID I!
BUT THEY ARE MADE MUCH AS WE!
YOU BEGIN TO SEE AS I DO... THE OLD BELIEFS AREN'T ALWAYS TRUE!
BIGTHINGS REMEMBER PETALWING?
OH! IT IS ONE OF THE GOOD SPIRITS!
THANK YOU AGAIN FOR SAVING US FROM MY FATHER!
YES! WE THANK YOU!

AYOOOOOOO
YAA
AYOOOOOAH! AYOOOAH!
MALAK! LISTEN!
WOLVES!
OH, TAM!
I HEAR, LEETAH!
COME ON! LET'S GO FIND THEM!
OOO! I KNOW WHO THAT IS!
HAH!
SO DO I, CUB, SO DO I!

AAAAAAAYOOOOOOOO

AAAAAAAAAAYOOOOOOOOOOOOOOAAAAHAYOOOOOAA

THE HOWLS COME FROM EVERY SIDE! WE MUST *RUN, SELAH!*

RUN OR *FIGHT!*

BUT OUR ONLY WEAPON IS *MY KNIFE!*

THEN DO NOT ARGUE, DAUGHTER OF CHIEFS!

RUN!

THEN *WHOSE* EYES BURN FROM THE BRANCHES AHEAD?
BY THE *DEATH WATER!*

AND WHO ATTACKS FROM *BEHIND?!*

GUIDED BY THE HOWLS THEY HAVE RECOGNIZED, CUTTER, LEETAH, SKYWISE AND THE TWINS ALL ARRIVE IN THE CLEARING AT THE SAME TIME!
SUNTOP! EMBER! STAY BACK!
GRRRR!
GO AWAY, TALL ONES!
OUR CALLS WERE NOT MEANT FOR YOU!
THERE ARE, INDEED, WOLVES IN THE BUSHES! BUT THERE IS SOMEONE ELSE, AS WELL! THE POWERFUL BOW IS OF REDLANCE'S SHAPING. NIGHTFALL DRAWS IT BACK WITH SLOW AND DEADLY AIM!
BEWILDERED AND FRIGHTENED, MALAK AND SELAH GAPE AT THE STRANGE, POINT-EARED BEINGS. WEAPONS AND WOLVES SURROUND THE YOUNG HUMANS ON ALL SIDES --

-- SAVE ONE!
NIGHTFALL! DON'T SHOOT!
LET THEM GO!
THE DAUGHTER OF OLBAR VANISHES WITH HER LOVER. IN YEARS TO COME SHE WILL TELL HER DAUGHTERS OF THE FORBIDDEN GROVE'S MANY MYSTERIES. BUT FOR NOW...SHE HAS SEEN ENOUGH!
MY CHIEF-FRIEND! WE'VE FOUND YOU! MY EYES SEE WITH JOY!
MY HAND TOUCHES WITH JOY! NIGHTFALL... REDLANCE!
IF I'VE BEEN HAPPIER TO SEE YOU TWO, I CAN'T REMEMBER WHEN!

OH *LEETAH!* WHEN YOUR MOUNT RAN AWAY WITH YOU, I *FEARED* FOR YOUR *LIFE!*

THANK THE *HIGH ONES* YOU'RE SA-- ?
EH?
WHAT'S THIS IN YOUR *HAIR?*

HEE HEE!
PETALWING HAPPY!!
GOT MANY HIGHTHINGS TO TAKE CARE OF NOW!

NEVER MIND ABOUT *THAT! WHAT ABOUT THE WOLF-RIDERS?!* AND THE *GIANT BIRDS?*

I WISH THE TALE WERE EASIER TO TELL, CUTTER...
BUT I'M AFRAID NIGHTFALL AND I WERE THE ONLY ONES TO ESCAPE THE GREAT BIRDS' ATTACK!
"THERE WAS NO WAY TO FIGHT THEM -- IT HAPPENED TOO FAST!"
"OUT IN THE OPEN, WE WERE AS HELPLESS AS FISH TRAPPED IN SHALLOW WATER!"
"ONE BY ONE THEY PLUCKED US UP FROM THE GROUND LIKE WORMS OFF A LOG!"
"THE BIRDS WENT AFTER STRONGBOW FIRST! WHEN MOONSHADE SAW HIM CARRIED INTO THE SKY --"
"-- SHE JUST STOOD THERE AND LET HERSELF BE TAKEN, TOO!"

"THE REST OF US TOOK WHAT COVER WE COULD! THE WATER WASN'T DEEP, BUT WE HOPED IT WAS DEEP ENOUGH THAT THE BIRDS COULDN'T DIVE DOWN AND SPEAR US WITH THEIR CLAWS!"
"NIGHTFALL AND I STAYED UNDER, HUGGING THE RIVER BED UNTIL WE ALMOST DROWNED! WE WERE SAFE, BUT OTHERS WEREN'T SO LUCKY!"
"LEETAH'S ZWOOT NEARLY TRAMPLED US WHEN WE CAME UP FOR AIR! ITS HOOVES KNOCKED US BACK BENEATH THE WATER!
WE RECOVERED AND DRAGGED OURSELVES TO THE RIVER BANK..."
"...BUT BY THEN THE MONSTERS WERE ALREADY FLYING AWAY WITH THEIR CATCH!"
"SEVEN BIRDS -- SEVEN OUT OF TEN WOLFRIDERS CAPTURED! WE COULDN'T FIND THE MISSING ONE!"

"IT TOOK US A WHILE TO DECIDE WHAT TO DO. ALL WE HAD LEFT WERE THE WOLVES --"
"-- AND THE KNOWLEDGE THAT LEETAH HAD ESCAPED WITH EMBER AND SUNTOP!"
"WE DECIDED TO TRACK THEM BECAUSE WE KNEW THAT SUNTOP COULD LEAD US TO YOU, CUTTER," REDLANCE FINISHES. "IT WAS JUST LUCK THAT YOU WERE NEAR ENOUGH TO HEAR US WHEN WE HOWLED FOR YOU!"
SCOUTER SAID HE THOUGHT HE GLIMPSED RIDERS ON THE BIRDS' BACKS. THAT MAY BE SO...
ALL I KNOW IS THAT OUR TRIBEFOLK ARE GONE!
GONE...

...TO THE LAIR OF THE BIRD SPIRITS!
WE WANTED TO GO TO THE BLUE MOUNTAIN... NOW WE HAVE TO GO!
NO!!
FATHER, DIDN'T YOU BELIEVE ME? DON'T YOU EVEN BELIEVE SAVAH?!
I TRIED TO GIVE YOU HER WARNING!
PLEASE! YOU MUSTN'T GO NEAR THAT MOUNTAIN!

YOU DID WELL, MY CUB...
SAVAH CAN BE PROUD OF YOU -- AS I AM!
BUT A WOLFRIDER FACES DANGER -- ESPECIALLY WHEN HIS TRIBE NEEDS HIS HELP! THAT'S ALL THAT MATTERS, SUNTOP --
"-- THE TRIBE!"

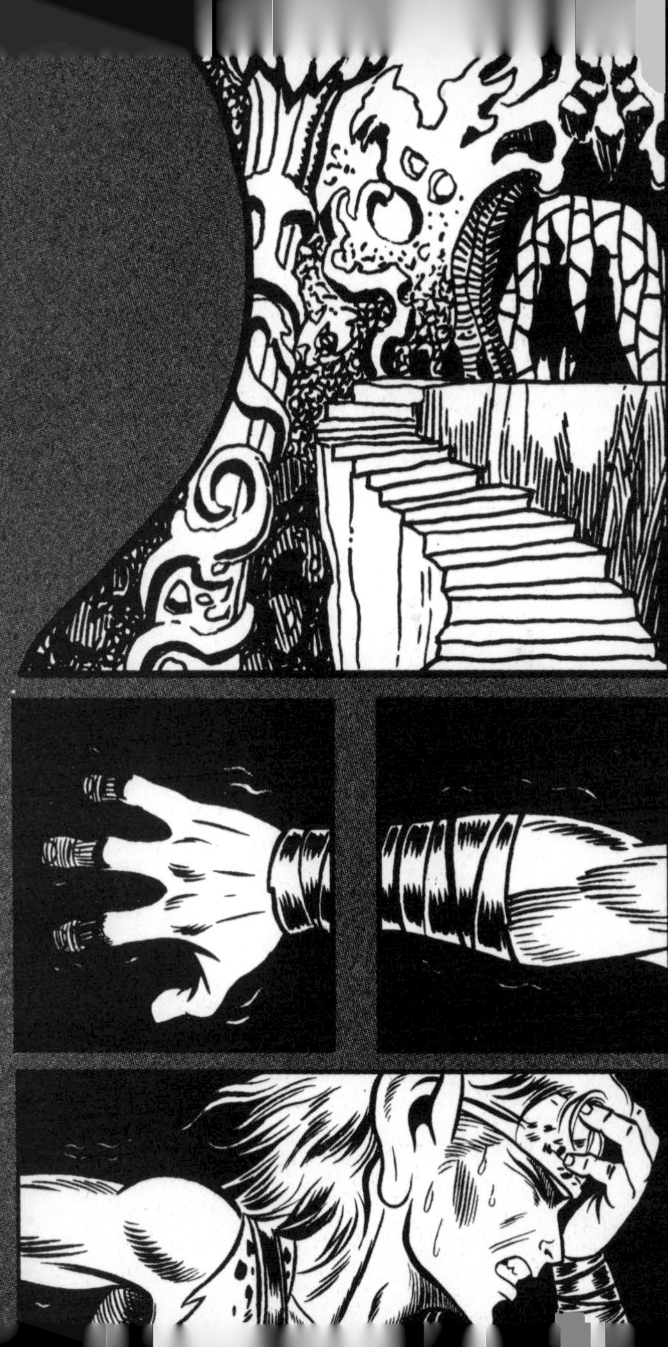

WINNOWILL?
NOT YET...
HE PLAYS THE GAME *WELL.*
BUT I SHALL WIN.
I ALWAYS DO!

LAIR OF THE BIRD SPIRITS

I FIND IT HARD TO BELIEVE THAT THESE SMALL *BRUTISH* CREATURES ARE IN ANY WAY RELATED TO US.
⁏SIGH⁏ DISAPPOINTING... PREDICTABLY UNIMAGINATIVE.

BUT THEY ARE, TYLDAK. ISN'T IT AMUSING? HOW LIKE FRANTIC BEASTS THEY SEEM.
BOTH HE AND HIS MATE WOULD REND US TO PIECES...IF THEY COULD!
SEE THIS SILENT ONE'S SHARP, TEARING TEETH?
SEE HOW HE SNARLS WITH RAGE?
LET HIM GO! LET HIM GO OR -- I'LL KILL YOU!!
AN INTERESTING CHALLENGE...
DO YOU THINK YOU CAN TAKE MY LIFE, LITTLE ONE --

-- BEFORE I TAKE *HIS*?
STOP!
STOP TORTURING HIM!
PLEASE!
OH, PLEASE STOP!!
HE *DESERVES* TO SUFFER FOR HIS CRIME!
SOB
STRONGBOW... MY LIFEMATE... *FORGIVE* ME!

AT THE MOUNTAIN'S BASE, A FAR MORE PEACEFUL SCENE TAKES PLACE.
THE MOONS ARE FULL, AND EACH WEARS A RING OF MISTY LIGHT! WILL THE STRANGE HONORED ONE SPEAK TO US TONIGHT, DO YOU THINK?
HE WILL NOT TAKE OUR OFFERINGS IF WE STAY AND WATCH FOR HIM...PATIENCE! BY AND BY HE WILL LET US KNOW HIS WILL!
I HAVE GLIMPSED HIM IN THE SHADOWS -- HE IS FIERCE TO BEHOLD, SURROUNDED BY GREAT BEASTS OF THE NIGHT!
HE DOES NOT FLY UPON A BOND-BIRD LIKE HIS FELLOWS. THAT IS STRANGE.
BUT WE MUST NOT QUESTION THE WAYS OF THE BIRD SPIRITS!
THEY HAVE SENT US A MESSENGER WHO WILL SPEAK TO US IN HIS OWN TIME --
-- AND IN HIS OWN WAY!
COME! THERE IS MUCH LEFT TO BE DONE FOR THE CEREMONY!

SNIFF
THREE NIGHTS IN A ROW AND THEY STILL HAVEN'T TRIED TO POISON US!
I COULD ALMOST BELIEVE THESE HUMANS MEAN US NO ILL!
HAH! THAT'LL BE THE DAY!
BUT FOOD IS FOOD, WHETHER WE HUNT IT OR STEAL IT, EH, FRIENDS?
AYE, SMOKE-TREADER!
THEY'RE UP THERE, ALL RIGHT...
CLEARBROOK, SCOUTER, AND THE OTHERS. I'D GIVE MY ONLY EYE --
-- TO KNOW HOW THEY FARE! BUT I DON'T DARE SEND!
THERE'S A POWERFUL ENEMY INSIDE THAT MOUNTAIN!
ONE WHO CAN BLOCK MY SENDING -- TURN IT AGAINST ME!
BUT DON'T WORRY, FRIEND!
SOMEHOW I'LL FIND A WAY TO FREE THE WOLF-RIDERS!
EH? SOMETHING ON THE WIND?
ONE-EYE WATCHES THE WOLVES CLOSELY. THE LANGUAGE OF THEIR BODIES IS ELOQUENT. SOMEONE IS COMING --
WHUF!

--SOMEONE WHO IS YET FAR AWAY...
BREE DEE DEE DREET DREET DEE EEE
DIRI DIRI BREEDEET DEEE
BREE DEE DEEDLE DREE
ENOUGH!
SCAVENGER BIRDS SING BETTER THAN THAT!
PETALWING SING VERY NICE!
HEY BUG!
OOO!
THERE'S A MOUSE ASLEEP IN THAT HOLLOW LOG -- GO WRAP IT UP!

IT WON'T WORK...
ANYTHING FOR A MOMENT'S PEACE!

GRRR!

BAD HIGHTHING FIBBED! WAS NO STILLQUIET FURSOFT CRADLEBABY THERE!
PETAL-WING VEXED!

NO YOU DON'T, BUG! THIS TIME I'M READY FOR YOU!

SPLOOZT!

YEEPH!

BLIBBER MOOFLE WHINE
CALMLY, TINY FRIEND. NOW IS NOT A GOOD TIME FOR SINGING!
LOOK AT FIRECOAT AND WOODSHAVER! THEY SENSE THE REST OF THE PACK SOMEWHERE IN THE DISTANCE.
THE WOLF-PACK WILL BE WHERE THE WOLFRIDERS ARE --
-- IF THE WOLFRIDERS LIVE!
THEY LIVE, NIGHTFALL! IF THEY WERE DEAD, WE'D FEEL IT! COME ON! WE'LL RUN LIKE DEER AND REACH BLUE MOUNTAIN BEFORE THE NIGHT'S HALF DONE!
PANT PANT CUTTER! W-WAIT!! I-I CAN'T...
WITHOUT BREAKING STRIDE, CUTTER SWEEPS LEETAH ONTO WOODSHAVER'S BACK!
NOW, MY GENTLE LEETAH... BE A WOLFRIDER!

THEY CALL THEMSELVES **HOAN G'TAY-SHO** WHICH MEANS "FAVORED OF THOSE WHO DWELL ON HIGH." **NONNA**, THE SYMBOL-MAKER, WAS ONCE A MEMBER OF THIS TRIBE, BEFORE HER MATE **ADAR** TOOK HER TO LIVE IN HIS OWN LAND. **NONNA'S** DEPARTURE CHANGED NOTHING -- FOR NOTHING CAN SWAY THE **HOAN G'TAY-SHO** FROM THEIR LONG CHOSEN PATH.

THE PIPES CALL LIKE THIN-THROATED BIRDS TO THOSE WHO DWELL HIGH ABOVE --

-- TELLING THEM OF AN **OFFERING** SOON TO ASCEND THE MOUNTAINSIDE.

ONE-EYE SPIES UPON THE HUMANS, UNAWARE THAT **HE** IS THE CAUSE OF THEIR PURPOSEFUL ACTIONS!

OUR LAST GIFT TO THE BIRD SPIRITS WAS ONE OF OLD AGE. TWO OF OUR ELDEST TRIBEFOLK CLIMBED THE STEEP PATH TO SPEND THE LIFE LEFT TO THEM WITH THE HONORED ONES... THE IMMORTAL BIRD SPIRITS WOULD KNOW US IN EVERY ASPECT AND CONDITION OF OUR BEING.
THEREFORE WE SEND THEM NOW A GIFT OF BEAUTY IN ALL ITS FULLNESS.
MAY THE HONORED ONES' MESSENGER, SILENT FOR THREE DAYS, KNOW BY THIS OFFERING THAT WE AWAIT HIS WORD!
THIS COULD BE MY ONLY CHANCE!
I'LL BET THAT CAVE IS AN ENTRANCE INTO THE MOUNTAIN! LOOKS TO ME LIKE IT'S WIDE OPEN TO THE HUMANS' USE... THAT MEANS IT'S WIDE OPEN TO ME!
MAYBE I CAN'T SCARE ALL THOSE BIRD-RIDERS BY MYSELF --
BUT WITH A PACK OF ANGRY WOLVES AT MY SIDE... HAH! THAT'LL MAKE 'EM THINK TWICE ABOUT HOLDING THE WOLFRIDERS PRISONERS!
ALL WE HAVE TO DO IS SCARE THE HUMANS ENOUGH TO GET PAST 'EM!
EH? WHAT'S UP?
RUFF R-R-RUFF!
WHINE
ONE-EYE KNOWS BETTER THAN TO IGNORE THE WOLVES, NO MATTER HOW URGENT THE NEED TO PUT HIS DARING PLAN INTO ACTION.
INSTINCTIVELY, HE TILTS HIS HEAD BACK AND CALLS...

ALMOST AT ONCE AN ANSWERING HOWL WAFTS UP FROM THE VALLEY...
AYOOOOOOOOOOAH!
BY TWO-SPEAR'S STONE POINTS!
THEY'RE ALIVE! ALIVE!!
ONE-EYE!
HA HAH! CURSE YOUR WAYWARD RUMPS, YOU FOOLHEADED CUBS!
SO HE'S THE MISSING ONE!
SO FAR!
SO! YOU TWO SURVIVED YOUR MAD QUEST AFTER ALL!
AND YOU WEREN'T CAPTURED BY THE GIANT BIRDS!

HUNH! NOT FOR LACK OF TRYING!
ONE OF 'EM GRABBED CLEARBROOK, SO I GRABBED HER.
BUT THAT OVERGROWN SQUIRREL-HAWK WAS SO STRONG, HE FLEW OFF WITH BOTH OF US!
CRASH!
MY WEIGHT MADE 'IM FLY LOW -- AND THAT WAS TOO BAD FOR ME!
I WOKE UP A LONG TIME LATER TO THE WOLVES HOWLING 'ROUND THE BASE OF THE TREE.
THE WOLFRIDERS... THEY'RE BEING HELD UP THERE IN THAT MOUNTAIN?
IN IT, LAD! MOUNTAIN'S HOLLOW!
THAT MUCH I LEARNED FROM MY ONE SENDING TO CLEARBROOK!
NO! DON'T TRY TO SEND -- ANY OF YOU!!
THE "BAD ONE" MUSTN'T LEARN HOW MANY OF US ARE STILL FREE!
THE "BAD ONE"?
SHH! WE'VE GOT EVEN MORE TROUBLE...

CAREFULLY THE ELVES CREEP TO A VANTAGE WHERE THEY CAN OBSERVE, UNSEEN, THE STRANGE CEREMONY OF THE HUMANS.

SKYWISE, LOOK! IT'S NONNA'S TRIBE! SEE HOW THEY'RE DRESSED?

I DO!

WE CAN ENTER THE MOUNTAIN THROUGH THAT TUNNEL UP THERE BUT FIRST WE'LL HAVE TO FIGHT OUR WAY PAST THOSE CURSED ROUND-EARS!

MAYBE NOT... WATCH THIS!

WHA--?!! GET BACK HERE!!

HE'S WALKING RIGHT UP TO THEM!?

THEY'LL KILL HIM!

I - I DON'T BELIEVE IT!

THE HUMANS...

THEY'RE BOWING!

AT THE SAME TIME, WITHIN THE MOUNTAIN...

HEAR THE *PIPES!*

I WONDER WHAT *PETS* THE HUMANS SEND ME NOW.

I WONDER THAT YOU NEVER TIRE OF TOYING WITH THE FIVE-FINGERED ONES!

AREN'T THESE SLAVES WHO CALL THEMSELVES THE *WOLFRIDERS* MORE AMUSING?

LISTEN! THE PIPES STOP! THAT IS ODD.
BUT NOW THEY RESUME.
BUT THE HUMANS ARE ENDLESSLY INTERESTING TO ME.
JUST WHEN I THINK I'VE OBSERVED EVERY POSSIBLE TRICK OF THEIR BEHAVIOR... THEY SURPRISE ME ANEW! I AM, AS YOU KNOW, MOST FOND OF SURPRISES.
GOOD! DOOR IS SO ATTUNED SHE WILL NOT FUNCTION WITHOUT THE PIPES. THE TIME HAS COME!
DOOR -- OPEN!

DOOR, A MYSTERIOUS, MOTIONLESS FIGURE ENTHRONED HIGH OVER-HEAD, DOES NOT ACKNOWLEDGE THE COMMAND BY ANY OUTWARD SIGN.
BUT BENEATH HER, THE WALL BEGINS TO SHUDDER, TO PULSATE AS STREAMS OF ROCK-SHAPING FORCE FLOW LIKE BLOOD THROUGH THE VEINS OF THE LIVING STONE!
SLOWLY THE ANCIENT WALL PARTS --
-- ITS SHAPE ALTERED BUT ITS MASS UNCHANGED.
AND THERE IN THE CORRIDOR BEYOND...
YOU!!
BIRD SPIRITS!

GIVE US BACK OUR TRIBEFOLK --
-- OR WE BITE WITH SWORDS AND FANGS!
WINNOWILL -- MORE SAVAGES! STOP THEM!
STARTLED FOR ONLY A MOMENT, THE DARK ROBED ELF WOMAN ACTS QUICKLY...
DOOR!
CLOSE!!
FOLLOW ME! HURRY!!
LOOK OUT!

AYOOOAH!!
HEE HEE!
FLYHIGHTHI
GOT BIG EYE
OOO!
A WINGED ELF!
HE'LL WARN HIS PEOPLE!
PETALWING! GO
AFTER HIM!

GAAH!!
CAN'T SEE --
CAN'T FLY!
WHERE ARE THE WOLFRIDERS?
HEE HEE!
AIIEE!!
ONE-EYE!
WHAT IS IT?
I - I TRIED TO SEND TO CLEARBROOK BUT THE PAIN IN MY HEAD, IT...
SHE -- SHE'S THE BAD ONE!!
OW!
I - I CAN'T SEND!
SHE'S TURNING MY THOUGHTS INTO KNIVES --
-- PIERCING ME WITH THEM!

LISTEN, ***FEATHER-ROBE...*** QUIT INTERFERING! I ***MEAN*** IT!

I BELIEVE YOU DO, SAVAGE...
I BELIEVE YOU DO!

FREE NOW TO SEEK OUT THEIR TRIBEFOLK IN THE CAVERNOUS LAIR OF THE BIRD SPIRITS, THE WOLFRIDERS SEND FORTH THEIR CALL!

TREESTUMP!

PLASH!

PIKE!

SCOUTER! DEWSHINE!

CLEARBROOK!

STRONGBOW! MOONSHADE!
:GASP!:
IT'S CUTTER! HE'S HERE!

HE'S HERE!!

AYOOOAH!

THERE'S MY CUB, FIT AND FINE AS EVER!
CUTTER! OH, CUTTER! THEY'VE PUT STRONGBOW IN A CAGE!

WHAT?!
MAKE THEM SET HIM FREE!

ARRRGH! MY ARM!

STOP HER!
HER POWERS! LIKE A HEALER TURNED INSIDE OUT! SHE *HURTS* RATHER THAN HEALS!
AARR!!
YII!

SUDDENLY, THE STRANGE WINGED ELF RETURNS!
TYLDAK! TAKE THEIR WEAPONS! SUBDUE THEM!
DOWN HE SWOOPS AT FULL SPEED -- AND NOT ALONE!

I CAN'T BELIEVE IT! THEY FLOAT UPON THE AIR!
SO THAT ANCIENT SKILL IS NOT LOST TO ELVES AFTER ALL!
TWUNG!
I'LL TRY TO WOUND...!
GASP!
HE SKIMS THROUGH THE AIR LIKE A WATER BUG ON A POND!

SNIK

MY BOW!
KLATCH!

DON'T WORRY! HIS TOY ON A STRING IS NO MATCH FOR A *SWORD!*

GET THE BLADE!
HEY!
LET GO!

HOLD STILL, YOU SKINNY HUMMINGBIRD!
CUTTER! WATCH YOUR BACK!
THANKS, PIKE!
I'M ENDING THIS GAME --
KLAT!
TAK!
--NOW!
UNH!

BRIERSTING! GO!!
TREESTUMP! LOOK OUT!
WHA --?
THE WARNING COMES A MOMENT TOO LATE...

KEEP THAT BLADE *WHIRLING,* LAD -- I'LL BE OUT OF THIS IN NO TIME!

IT GOES *BADLY!*
THE SAVAGES FIGHT AS THOUGH IT IS ALL THEY HAVE EVER DONE!

BUT *I* KNOW HOW TO TIP THE BALANCE!
THE COWARD! SHE'S GOING AFTER *STRONGBOW!*

WOLFRIDERS! FOLLOW MOONSHADE!
STRONGBOW MUST BE SOME-WHERE UP THESE STAIRS!
LET MY LIFEMATE BE, YOU BLACK SNAKE!
NO HUMAN WAS EVER AS CRUEL AS YOU!
I FAILED AGAINST YOU ONCE --

-- BUT I'M NOT ALONE *THIS* TIME!
GRRR!

STOP!

HAVE YOU FORGOTTEN?

WINNOWILL'S CRYPTIC WORDS BRING THE FORMER CAPTIVES TO AN INSTANT HALT...
WHAT'S THE *MATTER* WITH YOU --?!
FIGHT!

WOLFRIDERS!
DO AS CUTTER SAYS!
FORGET ABOUT ME!
STRONGBOW!
NO!
THIS IS MERELY
A REMINDER.

I HAVE THE POWER TO *SHATTER* YOUR FRIEND FROM WITHIN! PROVOKE ME FURTHER -- AND I *WILL DO IT!*

SH-SHE'S NOT LYING! WHAT CAN WE DO?

THIS IS WHY WE DIDN'T DARE REBEL BEFORE, LAD...

THAT *WINNOWILL* HOLDS *STRONGBOW'S* LIFE IN HER HANDS!

WINNOWILL...

WITHOUT WARNING, LEETAH DASHES TOWARD THE ELFIN ARCHER'S CELL!

STRONGBOW!

TAKE MY HAND!

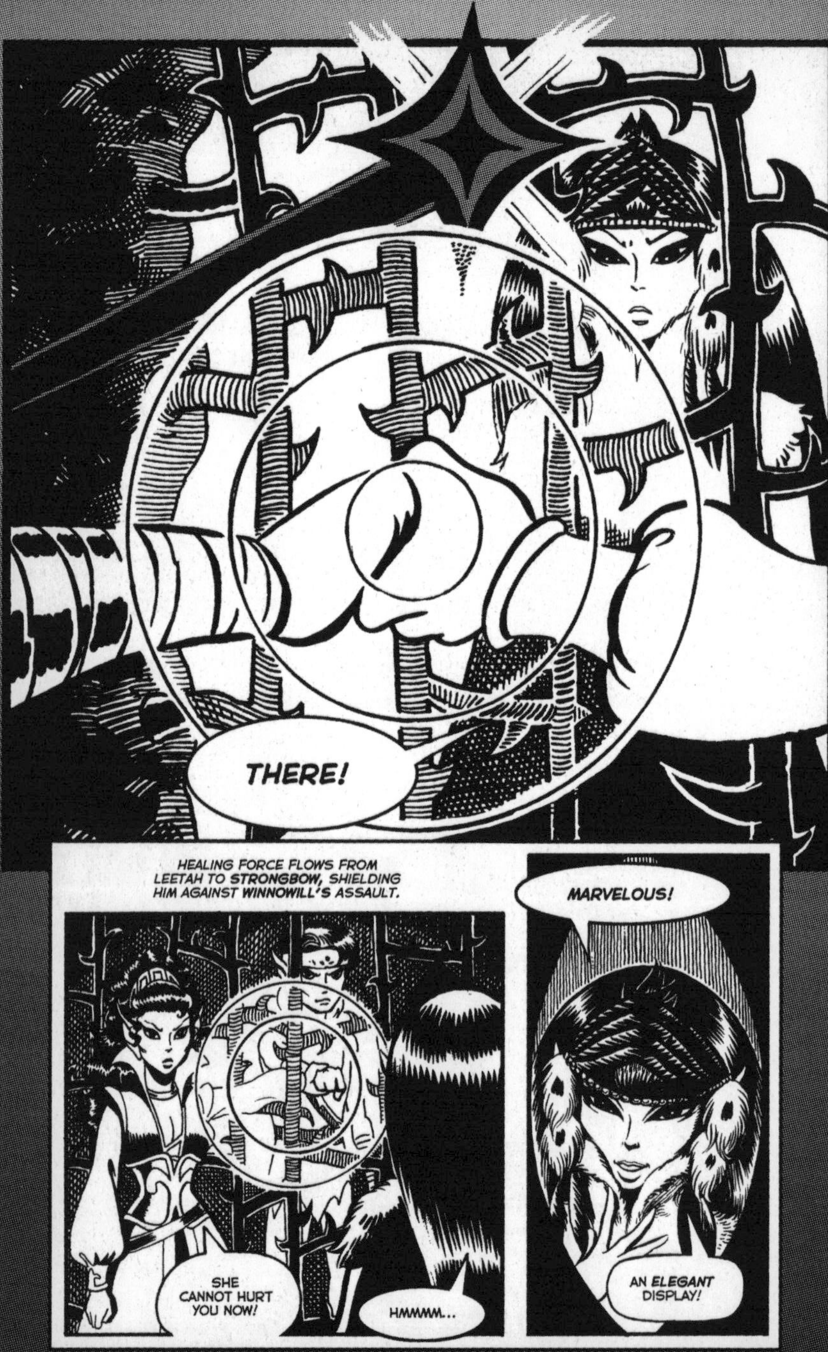

THERE!

HEALING FORCE FLOWS FROM LEETAH TO **STRONGBOW**, SHIELDING HIM AGAINST **WINNOWILL'S** ASSAULT.

SHE CANNOT HURT YOU NOW!
HMMMM...

MARVELOUS!
AN *ELEGANT* DISPLAY!

I SEE YOUR DISSIMILARITY TO YOUR COMPANIONS IS MORE THAN SKIN DEEP, MY DEAR.

WHY HAVE YOU ABUSED AND HUMILIATED THE WOLFRIDERS?

WHY HAVE YOU TAKEN AWAY THEIR FREEDOM?

BECAUSE THEY HAVE TAKEN THE LIFE OF A FLEDGLING -- A DESTINED BOND-BIRD OF THE GLIDERS!
THESE ATE OF ITS FLESH --
-- BUT THAT ONE SHOT THE FLEDGLING DOWN!
IT IS A CRIME FOR WHICH THEY MUST PAY!
WE WERE GIVEN A CHOICE... SERVE THE GLIDERS AS SLAVES, OR TAKE OUR FREEDOM IN EXCHANGE FOR STRONGBOW!
THAT'S NO CHOICE, TREESTUMP!
YOU DID THE ONLY THING YOU COULD, BUT IT'S OVER NOW!
WE'RE GETTING OUT OF HERE -- ALL OF US!
MY, MY! HOW OUR SCATTERED DESCENDENTS HAVE DEGEN-ERATED!
NOT ONLY HAVE THEIR BODIES SHRUNK --
-- THEIR SENSE OF HONOR SEEMS TO HAVE VANISHED COMPLETELY!

YOU, LITTLE CHIEFTAIN... *JUSTICE* IS MERELY A MATTER OF CONVENIENCE TO YOU, ISN'T IT?
WHAT'RE YOU TALKING ABOUT?
IF SOMEONE KILLED ONE OF YOUR WOLF-FRIENDS, WHAT WOULD YOU DO?

WHY, I'D *K*-- !

UH...

THAT WOULD DEPEND...

YOU WASTE MY TIME, FEATHER ROBE! I'LL TAKE THIS UP WITH YOUR CHIEF AND NO ONE ELSE!
WITH MY... CHIEF?
HOW QUAINTLY YOU PUT IT!
BY ALL MEANS LET US SET THIS MATTER BEFORE VOLL, LORD OF THE GLIDERS!
CUTTER?
HMM?
I THINK WE'RE UP TO OUR EARS IN BIRD PL--
-- UH HUH!
WELL, TAM... YOU FOUND WHT YOU'D HOPED YOU'D FIND.
THE "BIRD SPIRITS" ARE ELVES!
BUT SUNTOP'S WARNING WAS WELL WORTH HEEDING. THERE'S SOMETHING WRONG WITH THIS PLACE --
-- AND WITH THESE FOLKS WHO CALL THEMSELVES GLIDERS!

I'M GLAD SUNTOP AND EMBER ARE SAFE IN THE WOODS WITH REDLANCE!

DON'T SEND ANY MORE!
THAT PRYING SHE-FERRET CAN PICK YOUR THOUGHTS
RIGHT OUT OF THE AIR!

LED BY WINNOWILL, THE WOLFRIDERS VENTURE DEEP INTO THE BOWELS OF THE GLIDERS' MOUNTAIN DOMAIN...
POOR LITTLE PETALWING! IT MUST BE LOST SOMEWHERE IN THIS HUGE, CONFUSING PLACE!

DEEPER...
I'LL TELL YOU ONE THING -- THE TROLL CAVES WERE NEVER THIS FANCY!

STILL...
JOYLEAF... LET YOUR BLOOD FLOW STRONGER IN ME, NOW, THAN *BEARCLAW'S.*
KEEP ME CALM AND WISE BEFORE THIS *LORD VOLL.*
IT'S TIME TO *THINK* -- NOT TO *FIGHT!*
ONE-EYE!
CLEARBROOK!

THEY KEPT ME FROM GOING TO YOU! THEY TIED MY HANDS AND FEET!
BY THE TWO MOONS!
WHAT HAVE THEY *DONE* TO YOU?
CHUCKLE NOTHING, BELOVED... ***NOTHING!***

HE SEEMS EVEN OLDER THAN SAVAH!
A CLOAK MADE OF SO MANY YEARS MUST WEIGH HEAVILY ON HIM. HE WEARS IT WITHOUT JOY.
BOLDLY CUTTER STEPS TO THE FOOT OF VOLL'S ELABORATE PERCH. THE TWO LEADERS EYE EACH OTHER COOLLY.
I AM CUTTER, CHIEF OF THE WOLF-RIDERS.
I DEMAND THAT YOU RELEASE STRONGBOW AND LET ME AND MY TRIBE GO IN PEACE.
VOLL SUMMONS ONE OF THE GLIDERS TO THE DAIS...
THIS IS KUREEL.
YOUR FOLK KILLED THE FLEDGLING WHICH WOULD HAVE BECOME HIS BOND-BIRD.
I'M SORRY FOR THAT. WE'RE HUNTERS. STRONGBOW SHOT THE BIRD DOWN FOR FOOD.
HE DIDN'T KNOW.

THE CHOSEN EIGHT WHO RIDE THE GREAT BIRDS ARE HUNTERS TOO. BUT KUREEL MUST WAIT, NOW, FOR THE NEXT HATCHING.
AND WAIT LONGER STILL UNTIL HIS NEW MOUNT IS FULL-FLEDGED AND READY TO FLY THE HUNT.
THEN LET MY TRIBE GO AND WE'LL BRING YOU MEAT TO MAKE UP FOR THE BIRD'S DEATH.
THAT HARDLY SEEMS ADEQUATE ATONEMENT, LORD VOLL...
I WOULD SAY THAT A LIFE FOR A LIFE IS MORE IN ORDER!

I AGREE!
YOU WON'T KILL STRONGBOW!
THAT WAS NEVER MY INTENTION, YOUTH.
BUT THE ARCHER'S WOLF-FRIEND...
GASP BRIERSTING?!
NO!
A LIFE FOR A LIFE... IT IS ONLY JUST!
MY MOUNT WAS SLAIN WHILE TRYING ITS WINGS! WHY SHOULD THE KILLER'S MOUNT LIVE?
BECAUSE IT WAS AN ACCIDENT!!
WHY WON'T YOU LISTEN?

LORD VOLL, PLEASE! YOU CANNOT COMMAND US TO KILL THE WOLF!
LEETAH!
YOU MIGHT AS WELL COMMAND THAT WE PUT OUR OWN ***CHILDREN*** TO DEATH!

WHAT?!
COME HERE!

CHILDREN, YOU SAY?
I THOUGHT ONLY ***WINNOWILL*** WAS CAPABLE OF SUCH CRUEL MOCKERY!

THERE ARE NO MORE CHILDREN!
THERE WILL *BE* NO MORE!
WE ARE ALL *DYING* WITHIN THIS MOUNTAIN... DYING, THOUGH UNABLE TO DIE!
SURELY YOU HAVE SEEN THAT!
DESPITE THE RECENT BATTLE, *LEETAH'S* HEART IS TOUCHED BY THE AGED LEADER'S PAIN.
BUT THERE *ARE* ELF CHILDREN IN THE WORLD, *LORD VOLL!*
LITTLE ONES FULL OF STRENGTH AND PROMISE!

LITTLE ONES WHO HAVE KNOWN ONLY *RESPECT* AND *LOVE* ALL THEIR SHORT LIVES.
IF ONLY THAT WERE TRUE...AFTER ALL THIS TIME...I'D GIVE *ANYTHING* TO GAZE INTO THE EYES OF A CHILD --
-- JUST ONCE... TO FEEL *HOPE* AGAIN!
OH, *SUNTOP!* DON'T BE SUCH AN OLD *GLOOMER!*

I DIDN'T DO IT RIGHT!
I DIDN'T WARN FATHER THE WAY SAVAH WANTED ME TO!
NOW HE'S UP IN THE MOUNTAIN WHERE HE ISN'T SUPPOSED TO BE!
AWW...
FATHER WILL SAVE THE WOLF-RIDERS! HE CAN DO EVERYTHING!
NO ONE CAN DO "EVERYTHING" BY HIMSELF, EMBER. BUT WITH THE WOLFRIDERS FIGHTING BY HIS SIDE, THERE'S VERY LITTLE YOUR FATHER CAN'T DO!
OH LOOK!!
GIANT BIRDS!
TIMMORN'S BLOOD!

HIDE IN THE BUSHES, *QUICK!*
CRACKLE
REDLANCE!
EH?!
NO NEED FOR WARINESS, BELOVED!
I RIDE THE WIND ASTRIDE THE GREAT BIRD!
NIGHTFALL! IT'S NIGHTFALL!!
HA HAH!

MEET US AT OUR LANDING PLACE! BRING SUNTOP AND EMBER! THEY ARE NEEDED!
MEANWHILE, HIGH WITHIN THE TOPMOST PEAK OF BLUE MOUNTAIN...
I CANNOT RECALL HOW LONG IT HAS BEEN SINCE I LAST SET FOOT IN THIS AERIE.
ONCE, I FELT AS ONE WITH MY OWN BOND-BIRD AND SAW THE WHOLE WORLD SPREAD OUT LIKE A MANY-COLORED CLOAK FAR BELOW ME.
BUT THE PAST IS A CLOUD, EASILY SEEN FROM A DISTANCE --

-- MISTY AND INTANGIBLE WHEN I TRY TO GRASP IT...

THEY'RE RETURNING, LORD VOLL!
THE WOLFRIDERS TOLD THE TRUTH!

MOTHER! FATHER! DID YOU SEE? DID YOU SEE US FLY UP IN THE AIR?
WE SAW, EMBER!
FATHER! YOU'RE ALL RIGHT!
EVERYBODY'S ALL RIGHT!
THE BIG BIRD TOOK US UP SO HIGH -- WE SAW ALL THE HUMANS AND THEY WERE SMALL LIKE LITTLE SPECKS AND...
...GOT MY "MAGIC FEELING," MOTHER, BUT I'M NOT SCARED LIKE BEFORE...
WHO'S HE?
THIS IS LORD VOLL --
-- A FRIEND!

YOU LOOK LIKE A *FUNNY* OLD BIRD!

HEY!
BAP!
EMBER! HE'S LIKE *SAVAH!* BE POLITE!
WELL, *LORD VOLL...?*

YOU... DID NOT LIE!

NOW YOU WILL SEE THAT *MY* WORD IS EQUALLY HONORABLE.

STIFFLY, HIS RAGE AND HUMILIATION BARELY CONTAINED, A NEWLY-FREED **STRONGBOW** STRIDES INTO THE AERIE.

ONLY **BRIERSTING'S** HAPPY GREETING IS NOT DAMPENED BY THE TENSION IN THE AIR.

CUTTER, YOUR CHILDREN HAVE WON FREEDOM FOR YOU AND YOUR TRIBE.
THE CHOSEN EIGHT WILL TRANSPORT EACH OF YOU DOWN TO THE GROUND IF YOU WISH.

BUT I WANT --
-- I ASK THAT YOU STAY.
THE FLEDGLING'S DEATH WAS WORTHWHILE, FOR BY LUCKY CIRCUMSTANCE IT HAS BROUGHT ME PROOF OF OUR RACE'S RENEWAL!
I CAN'T SPEAK FOR MY TRIBE WITHOUT FIRST HOLDING COUNCIL, LORD VOLL. BUT FOR MYSELF, I WOULD CHOOSE TO STAY AND LEARN ALL I COULD OF THE GLIDERS.
THE WISEST ELF I KNOW ONCE SAID THAT OUR RACE IS OF "ONE HEART AND ONE MIND!"
I BELIEVE WE SHOULD ALL BE TOGETHER! IT'S MY DREAM TO FIND AND UNITE ALL THE LOST CHILDREN OF THE HIGH ONES.
THEN LOOK NO FURTHER, LITTLE CHIEFTAIN.
YOUR QUEST IS DONE.
WE ARE THE HIGH ONES!

IN THE NEXT VOLUME

Who are the tall, ancient elves who call themselves the Gliders, who have made labyrinthine Blue Mountain their home? And who is the seductive, mysterious Winnowill, whose enigmatic smile hides ten thousand years of illusion? Could the Gliders be the High Ones, the ancestors of all elves, including the Wolfriders?

Before Cutter can learn the answers to these questions, he will first see his tribe torn apart by the subtle evil that pervades Blue Mountain. And more, he will have to face a devastating revelation he could never have imagined — a secret that will change the course not only of his life, but also the lives of all his friends and kin.

Look for this latest addition in DC Comics' new library of ElfQuest stories in

AUGUST 2004